In Search of Willie Patterson

To the memory of my mother

Also by Fred Reid

Keir Hardie: The Making of a Socialist

In Search of
Willie Patterson

A Scottish Soldier in the Age of Imperialism

Fred Reid

Cualann Press

ISBN 0 9535036 7 4

First Edition 2002

British Library Cataloguing in Publication Data. A catalogue record of this book is available at the British Library.

Printed by Bell & Bain, Glasgow

Published by:

Cualann Press, 6 Corpach Drive, Dunfermline, KY12 7XG, Scotland
Tel/Fax 01383 733724
Email: cualann@btinternet.com Website: www.cualann.co.uk

Acknowledgements

When this book was almost finished, two works appeared which had important bearings on it. Hugh Strachan's *To Arms*, Volume I of *The First World War,* added greatly to our knowledge of the East African campaign and I have gratefully drawn on it, especially the section on the war in East Africa. Gary Sheffield's work helped me to place my grandfather's army service more firmly in the context of a 'forgotten victory'. If, in my conclusions, I am less up-beat about the British victory and continue to focus equally on the catastrophe which the war represented for European civilisation as a whole, that does not detract from the respect due to his vigorous and clear presentation of much recent scholarship.

In the course of research I accumulated debts too numerous to list here in full, but mention must be made of the following:

Mr Mike Bullock for sharing with me his great knowledge of British army signallers and Professor John Bourne for pointing me in the right direction in military history research; Mr M Coughlan, Lt Colonel, 1st Infantry Battalion, Irish Defence Force, for permission to visit Renmore Barracks, Galway, and Corporal Brian Smith, who guided me so knowledgeably round the museum; Mr George McIlrath of H A McIlrath and Sons, Estate Agents and Auctioneers, Kilrea, for sharing with me his knowledge of local history; Mrs Doreen Moreland of Kilrea Public Library for drawing my attention to many local sources and providing valuable photocopies. Mr Peter Barton of Kenilworth shared with me his knowledge of the East African campaign and allowed me to read in draft the relevant chapters of his biography of the flying ace, Leo Lwalmsley.

I also wish to thank the staff of the Mitchell Library, Glasgow, and of the British Library, London, for their never-failing support in tracing books and sources. The Register Offices of Scotland and Northern Ireland were prompt in their responses, and special mention must be made of the staff of Clydebank District Registration Office for help in teasing out the genealogical facts. Ms Pat Malcolm of Clydebank Public Library helped me with points of local history and referred me to the Post Office archive in London where I was again kindly assisted to obtain copies of William Patterson's record of service. Mrs Mary McAleer and Dr MacDonald of Clydebank High School helped me to trace records of my family in the school archive.

Dr Hilary Marland of the Department of History, University of Warwick, gave me helpful advice on medical records, as did Dr Alistair Tough of Glasgow University. Professor Alistair Fielder of Imperial College, London, and Ms Olga Miller of the Royal National Institute of the Blind kindly advised me on points relating to the history of venereal disease and ophthalmology.

My good friend Mark Pilbeam drew upon his Zimbabwean background to put me in touch with Karl Wolf, who guided me through East Africa with masterly skill and forbearance.

Marion Robertson, whose services to the working classes of Glasgow have been publicly recognised, provided many interesting memories of her early friendship with my mother, as did Mrs May Hutcheson of her later years. Mrs Margaret McQuire took photographs of relevant sites for me and tracked down several publications pertaining to Glasgow. Her husband, Alex, acted as an untiring and patient chauffeur during several visits to Glasgow archives. Likewise, my son Les, under great difficulties, drove me round the northern portion of Ireland to visit relevant sites. My daughter Julie accompanied us and also assisted me to track down several important sources at the National Newspaper Library, London.

My sister, Mrs Catherine Raeburn, read an early draft of the work and inspired me to think harder about its implications. Dr Robin Okey patiently listened to me going on about my ancestors and offered stimulating reflections. Dr Malcolm Hardman of Warwick University read a late draft and made many valuable suggestions for improving it. The final responsibility for the text is, nevertheless, mine alone.

Finally, I must thank my wife, Henrietta, who has put up with the intrusion of Willie Patterson into our lives for over three years. He has not been an easy guest and I am very grateful for her patience and understanding.

Fred Reid

21 April 2002

Biographical Note

Dr Fred Reid was born in 1937. At the age of fourteen he went blind and was subsequently educated at the Royal Blind School, Edinburgh. In 1962, he graduated from the University of Edinburgh with a first-class degree in History and went on to obtain his D.Phil. at the Queen's College, Oxford. In 1997, he retired as Senior Lecturer in History from Warwick University. His publications include *James Keir Hardie: The Making of a Socialist* and a number of essays on Thomas Hardy. He is married to a blind physiotherapist and together they have raised three sighted children.

The author at Namacura Station in Mozambique, 2000 (author)

Contents

Illustrations

Front Cover: The author and Antonio at an anthill near Nampula
Back Cover: Painting by Iain Hetherington

We aren't no thin red 'eroes, nor we
aren't no blackguards too,
But single men in barricks, most
remarkable like you;
An' if sometimes our conduct isn't all
your fancy paints,
Why, single men in barricks don't grow
into plaster saints ...

... For it's Tommy this, an' Tommy
that, an' 'Chuck him out, the brute!'
But it's 'Saviour of 'is country' when
the guns begin to shoot;
An' it's Tommy this, an' Tommy that,
an' anything you please;
An' Tommy ain't a bloomin' fool – you
bet that Tommy sees![*]

---

[*] Rudyard Kipling. *Tommy*

Foreword

Fred Reid's grandfather, Willie Patterson, was, as the extract from Kipling's Tommy suggests, no plaster saint, but then for much of his life he was one of Kipling's 'Tommy Atkins' serving in the army in the outposts of Empire. He was also a Glasgow man, born of Irish immigrant stock, and brought up in the crowded streets of the Calton district, where densely-packed housing squeezed in amid the smoke and noise and grime of industry. Willie Patterson's story is a personal story which is also the story of Glasgow. The army offered an escape from the dead-end of unskilled labour, but his calling to it also reflected Glasgow's enthusiasm for Empire. It was a city that had grown wealthy on imperial trade, from slavery, through tobacco, to cotton and locomotives. To defend India was to defend Scottish interests. Like many a Glasgow lad before and after, he at times found the army 'bull' difficult to take, but, at the same time, he thrived within its structures.

Civilian life for working people before the war – and indeed after – offered little security, and married life in a room and kitchen gave scant opportunity for easy marital relationships. But in 1914, Britain once again needed its 'thin red line of 'eroes' and Willie was off to East Africa to defend the Empire. But such imperial patriotism did not survive the First World War and the years of harsh depression that followed it. Those who had fought for the Empire and got little as a result, as Kipling had warned, 'ain't a bloomin fool – you bet that Tommy sees'. 'Tommy' had seen and Willie, like Glasgow, moved to the left in politics. In post-war Clydebank, there was the ILP for Willie and Socialist Sunday School and later the Young Communist League for his daughter. It was a journey taken by many in the west of Scotland, including the strong women who are also part of this story, and who had to make ends meet, maintain the home, bring up the family and survive, and whom the war too had helped find a voice.

History is about the personal and the unique but also about what these tell us about the wider world. Fred Reid brings the skills and insights of a professional historian to his family's tale. The piecing together of the tiny bits and pieces of records that survive for the Tommy Atkins of this world make a coherent story and the insights which allow him to set Willie Patterson's life in a wider context make this more than a family memoir. In Willie Patterson's struggles and misdemeanours, in the tensions and tragedies of his family life, in the difficulties of his relationships and in his political journey, one can find the story of working-class Glasgow. Fred Reid's is a remarkable book. Those with an enthusiasm for family history will find it a model of what can be done.

W Hamish Fraser
Professor of History at the University of Strathclyde

Chapter One

Motives and Bearings

'It's so soothing to be able to form a clear picture of things in one's mind. What is really terrible is what one cannot imagine.'[1]

The words of Marcel Proust give an immediate clue to my motives for writing this book. It is the life of my grandfather, William Flynn Patterson, or rather, as much of his life as I know. He was born in the slum district of Calton, Glasgow, in 1883 and died in 1953. I never met him and saw him, as far as I know, only once. That occasion was in Argyle Street. The busy Glasgow thoroughfare was crowded. Knots of window shoppers pressed around the plate glass windows of Boots the Chemist. Passers by jostled and dodged in and out of the throng. My mother and I made our way, with difficulty, through the crush. Suddenly she drew up short, like a horse refusing a jump, and muttered in her usual earthy speech, 'Christ! There's my bloody auld faither.'

'Where Mammy?' I asked, turning to follow the direction of her frowning gaze. A soldierly looking man, erect, silver haired, strode past and instantly disappeared among the crowds.

'Was that your Daddy?' I queried.

'Yes, but I don't want to talk about him.'

'Why not?'

'Never you mind. You wouldn't understand. You will when you're older.'

That was about the end of the Second World War when I was, say, seven or eight, and it was the first time I knew I had a grandfather

[1] Marcel Proust, Extract from *Swann's Way* from *Remembrance of Things Past published by Chatto & Windus.* Used by permission of the Estate of Marcel Proust, the translator and The Random House Group Limited. (Braille edition) 1966, XI, 66

on my mother's side. As she said, I did learn, not from anything she told me directly, but from listening attentively to the stories she repeated over the teacups to friends around our fireplace. As the evenings wore on, conversation would turn to the past. Her eyes would become hooded and her rosy complexion heighten as she spoke of her parents' married life.

Little pitchers have big ears and her tale stuck in my memory. She said that Willie Patterson had been a soldier who fought in the South African War – the Boer War she called it. He had returned to enter the Post Office, in which he became a sorter telegraphist in the Burgh of Clydebank. He had been extremely patriotic, she said, and kept his service medals hanging above the fireplace in their home.

Clydebank Town Hall, 1998 (Mrs Margaret McQuire)

Work in the Post Office could have been the foundation of a comfortable existence for Willie and his family had he not been a vicious womaniser. The Boer War had made matters worse, however, for Willie picked up syphilis during his military service in Africa. My mother was very explicit on this point. I remember her spelling out the categories of venereal disease as I concealed my attention behind a comic or a book which I was pretending to read, while avidly drinking in the details of grandfather's wicked ways. 'There's gonorrhoea and syphilis', she said, 'The worst is syphilis, and he had it.'

The heroine of my mother's tale was always Willie's wife, Sally, a strong woman who lived and strove for her family. As I grew up, I came to think of her as one who was driven into an early grave by a brutal husband who callously blighted her life and that of her children. But there were puzzling details in the story. The army, my mother said, had dealt with him on his return from the Boer War by taking him up to Maryhill barracks and 'sterilising him'. Yet I knew that he had fathered three children. And there were other puzzles. My mother remembered Willie as a 'great patriot', yet she also said that he had joined the Socialist movement on Clydeside after the First World War – an unusual conversion perhaps.

Another detail became puzzling when I started to write down for this book my memories of family tradition and gossip. How could my grandmother have married Willie Patterson on his return from the Boer War, as my mother's account implied? Working back from the known year of my grandmother's death, 1936, I realised that she would have to have been about eleven years old when she married. So I tracked down her marriage certificate and a whole new vista opened up. Willie Patterson was twenty-seven when he married Sally in 1911 – too young to have had much of a career in the Boer War, and certainly not one that produced medals, for that conflict ended in 1902, when Willie was little over eighteen. But a greater surprise came from my mother's birth certificate in which my grandfather entered his rank in 1916 as 'Lance-Corporal Royal Engineers Signal Service'. So he had served in the First World War! Why had my mother never mentioned that? How could she have got these wars confused? Had my grandfather ever been in Africa at all?

Here was a mystery which any historian would find irresistible. I extracted Willie's service record from the Ministry of Defence in London. From this I learned more intriguing facts. It became apparent that he had had two episodes of military service, not one: the first in Ireland and India, from 1902 to 1910, and the second in East Africa during the First World War. In the latter action he was decorated with the Military Medal, 'in recognition of conspicuous gallantry in action and devotion to duty'. There must, I concluded, be a good deal more to Willie than my mother had known and it began to seem almost a duty to put the record straight.

So began two years of detective work, following up clues in the genealogical record, the archive of the British Post Office and the writings of many historians on topics as diverse as the insurance industry, the public health of nineteenth century Glasgow and the life of rank-and-file soldiers in the Indian army. These were new adventures for me, for my work as a professional historian had had far more to do with the opponents of war, like Keir Hardie, than with the 'uniformed working class' and its life of barracks and camps. And there was an even greater novelty in that this is the first piece of historical writing I have undertaken through the new communications technology. As a blind historian, I had formerly to rely on the long and laborious process of gathering information slowly from people reading to me. I have been able to research this book more quickly by listening to printed works read by an electronic scanner. Even manuscripts, which scanners cannot yet decipher, were made more readily available through email and the assistance of helpful archivists. It is very much to be hoped that all research libraries will proceed quickly to join those which, like the British Library and the Mitchell Library in Glasgow, have installed this assistive technology.

As I immersed myself in books about the First World War, the little known campaign in East Africa began to fascinate me. I got a clear picture of it from historians like Hugh Strachan, but I began to feel that reading would not do by itself. Somehow I must get out to Tanzania, where Willie was stationed at first, and then to Mozambique, to stand on the battlefield where he won his military medal. This was at a place called Medo, but it was not marked precisely on maps of Mozambique, either of the past or the present.

But how to get there? A conventional holiday tour would hardly do. I knew enough to understand that northern Mozambique was decidedly off limits for the tourist industry. Had not Princess Diana visited it in her campaign for the clearance of minefields, sown there in the savage civil war of the 1980s? Even a princess couldn't have got them cleared away that quickly!

In chapter six of this book, I tell how I solved this problem and of my fascinating safari around East Africa with the remarkable Karl Wolf.

By means of these strenuous, yet very enjoyable exertions, I have been able to recover many facts unknown to my mother and correct some of her misconceptions. Willie Patterson's story is not a very edifying one, but I think it is a rather more honourable one than she believed.

As I worked to put the record straight, I found another and wholly unexpected satisfaction. Confronting Willie's story seriously for the first time raised a suspicion in my mind that my blindness (never explained by medical science) might have been a result of his venereal disease. Inquiry among professionals in the field of ophthalmology has assured me that this was never a possibility. This is at least one sin for which Willie need not answer.

* * * * * *

So much for my own motives. Willie's story, I suggest, has more than a personal or family interest, for it bears on a number of questions of interest to social historians. Many of these relate to military history, which has now, thankfully, advanced far beyond the 'drum and trumpet' stage to ask about the lives of ordinary men in the ranks. Why, for instance, did young men from the slums of industrial cities like Glasgow join the army? Willie's motives cannot be uncovered directly, but his actions suggest a rather careful balancing of considerations, a combination of patriotism with self-interest.

Again, it has not been usual to think of the British regular army of the early twentieth century as a school for self-improvement, yet it proved to be just that in Willie's case, raising him eventually from the ranks of unskilled labour to clerical employment as a sorter/telegraphist in the British Post Office.

The darker side of his story, relating to venereal disease, is also of more than personal interest. Thanks to the work of historians like Ronald Hyam, we know a good deal more than we used to about the sexual history of soldiering in the British Empire. It is not a pretty story. As Kipling knew, men who caught clap in the army were neither plaster saints nor blackguards, but ordinary men 'most remarkable like you'. We know now how the army callously placed young men in the way of temptation without offering any guidance or protection in the way of safe sex. Yet much in this topic remains obscure. Little, as yet, has been said about the treatment of the unfortunate men who became infected, though the disgraceful story of the treatment of women is rather better known. It is often assumed that there was no effective treatment for syphilis, yet my grandfather seems indeed to have been cured by treatment in a specialised military hospital.

On many other aspects of soldiers' lives, Willie's story sheds little new light. I have therefore relied heavily on the memoirs of serving soldiers and the works of new military history to reconstruct a picture of his experience, both in India and in East Africa. Yet there is one point on which Willie's story provokes reconsideration, or at least further reflection. This is the question of class tension within the regular army. The new military history seems to assume that it did not exist. John Bourne has written in a very stimulating study of the subject: 'The army's method with recruits was to divest them of their civilian values and recreate them in the army's image.' They were able, he argued, to do this relatively easily. Young and impressionable men from the poorest and least educated ranks of the working class were separated from their families and cultures; the focus of their lives became the regiment. As other military historians have argued, the regiment was like a new family. It housed, fed, clothed and instructed the recruits and they learned to look up to their superiors as public school boys learned to respect their masters.

Willie's first regiment, the Connaught Rangers, did indeed offer such indoctrination and no doubt it worked to a considerable extent. Yet his story suggests that the private soldier, even in the pre-war regular army, could have his own agenda of aspirations and goals. Willie wanted something for himself out of military service – training in a skill and transfer to a skilled job in civilian life. He also came to want a pension at the end of the service he evidently gave with considerable commitment. Civilian life took an unconscionable time to deliver the skilled job and the army failed him in respect of the pension. He did not submit silently, however, to cold, impersonal, bureaucratic treatment. On the matter of the pension, he appealed beyond his regiment to the War Office. True, his protest was brushed aside, but it is the fact of it which suggests that 'rankers' were not always the malleable toy soldiers which the army wished to mould.

In addition, there is the question which feminists have raised since the days of Mary Wollstonecraft regarding the masculinity inculcated by the military code. On the basis of my mother's memories we might assume that Willie fitted readily into Wollstonecraft's stereotype: '… every corps is a chain of despots, who, submitting and tyrannizing without exercising their reason, become dead-weights of vice and folly on the community'.[2]

Yet even here, as I try to suggest, there may be another side to the picture. Willie, it seems to me, was as much a victim of his times as Sally. Nothing in their contemporary culture offered them much support in repairing the damage to their relationship which Willie's unfortunate sexual history inflicted. Each seems to have moved to an attitude of confrontation without considering or attempting negotiation and settlement. I do not wish to be misunderstood on this point. No one today would expect that Sally should have 'kissed the rod', though there was much in the culture of her time which counselled wives to do just that. But Willie, we should remember, passed on his ailment neither to his children, nor to his wife. His cruel reaction to Sally's understandable resentment suggests that he felt slighted and unjustly condemned. A wiser view of marital relations than was generally available at the time might have rescued the couple and their children from the bitterness and estrangement that blighted the lives of Sally and my mother.

* * * * * *

In the last analysis, then, this book attempts to make connections between my family history and other historical contexts. Ideally,

---

[2] Mary Wollstonecraft, *A Vindication of the Rights of Woman* (first published 1792, Penguin Classics edition 1985, edited with introduction by M Brody) p. 97

family history of this kind should be grounded in personal sources such as letters, diaries and the like. As will be seen, almost nothing of this kind has survived. I have been able to fill the gap to some extent from personal memories and (now and then significantly) from documents. I am fully aware, however, that the evidence of the actors' inner consciousness remains thin. Nevertheless, I trust my efforts will not be judged in vain. They may stand alongside better efforts of others as a model for family historians. It is practically certain that many family records remain to be extricated from old shoeboxes or suitcases and that those who possess them often feel that they are too 'trivial' to be of historical interest. If this book gives them confidence to inquire more fully into the question, it will have fulfilled one of my hopes.

I also wish to acknowledge that I have been forced by lack of evidence into a certain amount of speculation, notably on Willie's childhood and his turn towards Socialism in the 1920s. I have striven to show this clearly, so that readers will be able to discern it readily where it occurs.

I would also defend my right to speculate. There is speculation that is ungrounded and indefensible in historical terms. There is also speculation that is given significance by careful attention to the context of known facts. I have striven throughout to reconstruct the various contexts in which Willie lived out his relationships. To set Willie precisely within the known history of Glasgow, or the British army, or the Post Office, is to bring him forward from the shadows of memory and the dust of bureaucratic archives and construct a living man whose actions, if not excusable, are at least intelligible.

In attempting this, I have called finally to my assistance one of his great contemporaries, the novelist Thomas Hardy. In some respects, the novelist may see more deeply into the underground stream of private feeling than most of his or her contemporaries. In his novel *The Mayor of Casterbridge*, it seems to me that Hardy showed a penetrating understanding of what historians today call the 'new masculinity' and its relation to an age of Imperialism such as Britain went through during his novel-writing career. To see the parallels between the stories of Willie and of Michael Henchard, the mayor of

Casterbridge, is to find a framework in which the story of the former can be recreated as a subject for history and faithfully told.

This framework is, as I have said, the 'Age of Imperialism'. I make no apology for stressing it as the ultimate shaping force in the lives of my grandparents, but some words of explanation seem called for. I am not arguing that the First World War was caused by economic forces such as those depicted by Lenin in *Imperialism: the Highest Stage of Capitalism*. My point is, rather, that Willie especially played out his life at a time when 'Imperialism' was emerging more strongly in British culture and politics than it had done for, perhaps, a hundred years. By the time Willie went to war in 1914, few doubted that the defence of the Empire was as much an interest of Britain as the balance of power on the continent. Indeed, the two interests seemed intimately connected. The dominions and colonies supplied nearly one third of British food and raw materials for manufacture. Over half of British exports of cotton and iron goods went to the Empire and millions of British people (a disproportionate number of them Scots) migrated to the colonies. One quarter of the world was painted red on the map and a fifth of its population lived under British rule.

Such an Empire seemed worth fighting for in 1914, and, as a result of the fighting, was even larger after the First World War than it had been before. One of the new colonies wrested from other Empires was German East Africa, in fighting for which my grandfather won his Military Medal, a decoration of which he was extremely proud. At least my mother indicated that he was, and spoke scathingly of his patriotism. My reassessment of her judgment has, in the final analysis therefore, led me into a personal reassessment of British Imperialism as a historical fact and of the profession of arms from an ethical standpoint. Some of my conclusions would surprise and irritate my mother if she could read them today. In some ways they surprise myself, but I do not think they will surprise many other historians.

Chapter Two

Lum Hats and Music Halls

' ... I was only beginning to learn that life, for the majority of the population, is an unlovely struggle against unfair odds, culminating in a cheap funeral'.[3]

The first context to influence the making of my grandfather's personality was Calton, a densely overcrowded district lying just to the east of Glasgow's ancient 'Cross'. In the year of his birth, 1883, it was notorious for dirt, disease and criminality. This was not because 'Caltonians' were worse than the general run of humanity. It was, rather, the result of market forces, which, over the previous hundred years, had transformed a rural village into an industrial black hole.

So foul were its many common lodging houses that one social investigator wanted to place above their entrances Dante's famous inscription over the entrance to hell: 'All hope abandon ye who enter here.'[4] What the Victorians called 'vital statistics' told the same story more prosaically. Calton had more one-roomed dwellings, and more overcrowded houses, than almost any other district in Glasgow. Nearly twice as many children died in their first year in Calton, as compared to the middle-class district of Langside lying south of the river Clyde.

To this grim district had come, around 1870, an Ulster Protestant labourer called Clark Patterson. He left Ulster about 1860 with his wife Mary and infant son, Joseph. Taking the short crossing to the Clyde, Clark moved from one job in the building trade to another, working his way across Glasgow until he finally settled in

---

[3] S Sassoon, *The Complete Memoirs of George Sherston (London 1972) p.425.*
Reprinted by permission of Faber and Faber Ltd
[4] P Fyfe, *A Tour in the Calton*, p. 270

Calton, at number 17 Green Street. There he worked as a coal stoker and provided for the children Mary bore.

Backland, 75 Green Street (no photo of No 17 available) (Glasgow Museums)

In 1878, his eldest child, Joseph, married a Scots woman called Margaret Reid, and took her to live in a one-roomed house up the same tenement 'close' as his father. They had eight children whose births have been traced, of whom the third was my grandfather, Willie. He was born on 6 October 1883 and lived with his parents in and around Calton until he joined the army in 1902.

What was it like for Willie growing up in Calton during those closing decades of the nineteenth century? None of the Pattersons has left us any direct answer to this question. No letters or diaries survive, no family tradition dates from that remote time. Yet some kind of answer can be found by setting the lives of these Ulster Presbyterians in a context reconstructed from documents and the testimonies of contemporary witnesses.

Green Street (marked in black)

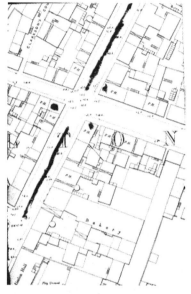

An Ordnance Survey map dating from Willie's boyhood shows that Green Street (marked in black on the map) lay in the thick of heavy industry. Immediately to the north of the Patterson home stood the Star Engine Works. To the west, a very large brick work. Round the corner, in Thomson's Lane, a coal yard and, at the southern end of the street, a carpet factory. Witnesses testify to the smoke that belched day and night from the tall chimneys of the works, covering every building with a black pall of soot and grime. The main thoroughfares were crammed with vehicles making for the City Centre or the outlying suburbs. Huge steam-driven lorries rumbled, hissing like fiery dragons, from the factory gates. Iron-shod wheels and hooves added to the din, rattling over cobbled streets with massive loads.

Number 17, where two generations of Pattersons lived, cannot be located on the map precisely, but was probably on the north-east side of Green Street, opposite the square of tenement buildings bounded by Kirk Street, Green Street, Moncur Street and Claythorn Street. This little complex of streets was the product of the City of Glasgow Improvement Act of 1866, which had provided for slum clearance and the construction of new tenements as 'hollow' squares, so arranged as to provide fresh air and washhouses in the 'back courts'.

But the good intentions of the city improvers had been undermined by the lack of strong planning regulations. As a result, when Willie was growing up, the square, which should have been open to the light, was actually crammed with a miniature shantytown of rickety wooden structures, thrown up hastily, to get rent from the poorest people of the district who could ill-afford the cost of the improved houses. The destruction of many houses to make way for railways, and the onset of economic depression in the 1870s, made overcrowding worse. Landlords met the housing needs of these poor people by partitioning larger rooms in the new improved tenements – 'making down' as it was called – and, when these were crammed to capacity, swallowed the overflow in the 'backlands'.

Green Street, looking north (Glasgow Museums)

It was in such streets that social investigators of the time found the worst conditions and the poorest families. One of these was Dr Russell, Medical Officer of Health for Glasgow, who prowled around the slum districts, ferreting out the truth and communicating it to audiences in the fashionable philosophical and literary societies of the city. Backland building, he told them, had produced slums every bit as overcrowded and uninhabitable as anything that existed before. Finding a particular dwelling in Calton was like exploration in darkest Africa. The sanitary inspector, guided by a postal address, found himself at a close which, however, proved to serve only as a front for a labyrinth of 'backlands', with no end of turnpikes, stairs, flats, and lobbies. The address then becomes something like this: Bridgegate, 10. 29, backland, stair first left, 3 up, right lobby, door facing!'[5] Mistakes were very frequent: 'You may find yourself at the door of a shop, or there may be no such number in the street, or no such person discoverable at the number given.'[6]

Like Charles Dickens, Russell wished to shock his polite audiences, confronting them, not only with the atrocious housing of the poor, but also with the social evils that flourished there. At times, his lectures read as though he is as much concerned to condemn the inhabitants as the houses:

> *One comes to know the lair of the criminal. It is always the back land where watch is readily kept, where defence is easy and attack difficult, where shame is unknown and honour is of the quality which prevails among thieves. When at noonday you find all the men about playing cards or loafing in the closes and on stairs, and superfluous women lolling over windows or nursing black eyes in corners, you can have no doubt of the calling of the inhabitants.*[7]

Russell painted a bleak picture of the children who grew up in these slums. Their health was his chief concern:

---

[5] J B Russell, Public Health Administration in Glasgow: a Memorial Volume of the Writings of James Burn Russell, Ed. A K Chalmers (Glasgow, 1905) p. 209
[6] Russell, pp. 209-10
[7] Russell, p. 235.

... consider the circumstances of poor children in such tenements. Raised above the street level to such a height and separated from such scant and dangerous room for play and exercise as those streets and courts afford, by dark lobbies and steep dark stairs, what can the poor things do? The playground of most of ... [them] ... below five years of age is the lobby and the stairhead. It is a sorry thing to hear their voices, and to feel them, for often you cannot see them, running about or sitting in groups in such places. No wonder that they are deformed with rickets and prematurely aged ... [8]

As children grew, they were turned loose to play and roam in the streets. 'Gutter boys' were a particular horror for Russell:

Probably the Glasgow boy is the wildest, most destructive specimen of a boy in existence and why? It is a law of child-nature to be constantly moving, constantly doing something. And what can a poor boy do in Glasgow but pull the bricks out of the walls of the ash pits; or climb on to the roof and tear off the slates? The landlords complain that the police do not protect their property. If they would not be so greedy of the soil, but provide more space for innocent games, the evil would be cured.[9]

Willie must have grown up in this way, playing with his brothers and sisters in the lobbies and stairheads and then learning to climb fearlessly on the ash pits and roofs. It is easy to understand why investigators like Russell regarded them as 'roughs', marking them off from the 'respectable' working class of the East End. But the social boundary was more fluid. Working-class family life had its own standards and constraints which the investigators often failed to appreciate. Mothers looking down from their windows, for instance, were not always idling. They were often guarding the children in the street – their own and others. Their sharp cries would nip bullying in the bud before it got out of hand. Their watchful gaze would pick out

---

[8] Russell, p. 105
[9] Russell, pp. 201-2.

any man who might be showing a lewd interest in the little girls or boys.[10]

Glasgow Green Children's Playground (Glasgow Museums)

Behind the windows in the one and two-roomed houses with their growing crowd of children, discipline was often strong. Mothers and older children restrained disorder among the younger ones. Father's heavy hand, slipper or belt, was often a sanction of last resort. Individuality could scarcely flourish. There was nowhere to be private and little scope for anyone to distinguish himself. Toys were makeshift and clothes were handed down from one child to the next. Everything had to be similarly shared.

In such circumstances, it was rare for anyone to feel himself singled out by destiny. Most people were fatalistic, rather, accepting

---

[10] This evidence comes from London's East End, but Glasgow sources attest to similar behaviour. See A Davin, *Growing up Poor: Home, Street and School in London,* 1870-1914 (London, 1996). Compare C Hanley, *Dancing in the Streets*

privation, and the occasional blow-out if father's horse came up, as lots bestowed indifferently by fortune.

Ambition was not entirely a stranger in Calton, however. It was often to be found among those who struggled to maintain their position on the margin of respectability above the 'roughs'. Such people often defined their community more by religion than by class. This seems to have been true, at least to some extent, of the first two Patterson generations. We can glean as much from genealogical, church and census records. Even such scant and fleeting entries reveal, when set in context, some fundamental facts of their lives: Irish origin; genteel poverty; evangelical Protestantism.

The Protestantism was a direct inheritance from Clark and Mary Patterson. The name means 'son of Patrick', suggesting a Catholic allegiance. At some time, however, Clark's ancestors must have conformed to the Protestant faith, for he married in the Presbyterian Church at Kilrea, County Londonderry, in 1855. Kilrea was then a thrusting market town in the vicinity of Coleraine. The linen industry had saved its agricultural poor from the worst ravages of the Irish potato famine. But in the late 1850s, hand loom weaving declined, and many of the younger working people sought escape through emigration. Most went to North America, but many, like Clark, made for the industrial cities of Britain. As we have seen, Clark and Mary settled in Calton, probably in the late 1860s, about the time of the City Improvement Act.

Mention of Ulster inevitably arouses thoughts of 'Orange' and 'Green' conflict, but these are not the associations which moulded the family ethos of Clark and Mary. They are to be sought instead in the evangelical tradition, which eschewed the violence of religious faction and the drunkenness with which it was often associated.

Evangelical preaching was a marked feature of Protestantism in Kilrea. The place was notorious for heavy drinking. In the time of Clark and Mary, it had no fewer than thirteen public houses for a population of below one thousand. The Ordnance Survey of Ireland stated in 1835 that 'Drunkenness and dram drinking prevails (sic) to a ruinous extent among all.'[11] The Presbyterian elite had long regarded this as a scandal and strove to instil godly behaviour in the brethren. A rigid Sabbath observance was demanded. Idleness on the Lord's Day was condemned. So were innocent pastimes like visits to friends and neighbours, 'carnal conversation' on the way to and from church, along with less innocent pursuits like parading with martial music and military exercises.[12]

Around the time of Clark and Mary's marriage, an event occurred which powerfully reinforced such puritanical sentiments. This was the 'second evangelical awakening' of 1859, imported from the United States. It took root in the district around Coleraine, where Clark and Mary lived. The first aim of the Gospel preacher was to humble the sinner before the Lord by inculcating a low sense of self-esteem. Young people flocked to prayer meetings, where the intensity of the experience often produced hysterical behaviour. Participants threw themselves prostrate on the floor, bemoaning past sins. The preachers attributed their shame to drunkenness and loose living.[13] Conversion and obedience to Christ were urged as the only sure foundation for prosperity in this world and the next. As the Presbyterian minister of Kilrea recorded:

> The '59 Revival movement touched the congregation deeply and a great improvement was reported in many ways – in attendance on the weekly union prayer meeting, in the number of communicants, and in general morals.[14]

People affected by this kind of evangelicalism were likely to be quietist in religion and politics, sober and industrious in their habits. Not for Clark and Mary the bitter, drunken strife of Orangemen and Fenians, so marked a feature of Saturday nights at Calton Cross. They lived quietly and decently, and identified with the most

---

[11] Extracts from the Ordnance Survey Memoir for the Parish of Kilrea, Co Londonderry, p. 32, Mic 6/230 (Kilrea Study Pack)
[12] J W Kernohan, *A History of Two Parishes: Kilrea and Tamlaght O'Crilly* (Coleraine, 1920) p. 62
[13] Kilrea Study Pack
[14] Kernohan, *Two Parishes*, p. 36

evangelical side of Scottish Presbyterianism. So much is suggested, at least, by the marriage of their eldest son, Joseph 'according to the forms of the Free Church of Scotland'.[15]

The Free Church had been formed in 1843, when middle class Presbyterians walked out of 'The Kirk', spurning the patronage by which landowners controlled the appointment of its ministers. It resembled Ulster Presbyterianism in this hostility to patronage, and in its openness to evangelical influences. In the 1870s it gave a warm welcome to a new wave of evangelical revivalism led by the American preachers, Moody and Sankey, from which arose in Calton the famous mission station known (from its beginning under canvas) as the Tent Hall.

Joseph married early, by the standards of the day, at twenty years of age. His wife, Margaret Reid, was the girl who lived next door or, more strictly, up the same tenement 'close' at number 17 Green Street. At twenty, she was not much below the average age of brides in Scotland, yet most middle class Victorians would have regarded this as an 'improvident' marriage. It probably did not seem like that to the young couple themselves. Joseph had done better than his father, thanks to the literacy which the self-improving Ulsterman had somehow acquired for his son. He was therefore able to work, not as an unskilled manual labourer, but as a china packer in the earthenware industry which had sprung up in Calton in the second half of the nineteenth century. The growing ranks of skilled workers could afford modern household articles, both necessities like toilet bowls and little luxuries like china teapots. Pottery had thus done something to cushion Calton against the decline of its textile industry and Joseph might well have felt himself abreast of the times.

But the collapse of the City of Glasgow Bank in 1878 interrupted the building of new houses and intensified the economic depression of the mid-1880s. Records show that 'china packers' were among the unemployed who had to be relieved by charitable soup kitchens in 1883.[16]

---

[15] Extract of an entry in the register of marriages, 34047, Number 408
[16] W H Fraser and R J Morris (eds) *People and Society in Scotland, 1830-1914* (Edinburgh 1990) p. 170

By this time, Joseph and Margaret had three children, of which the latest arrival was Willie. It would hardly be surprising, given the Ulster background, if they had turned to the church for help when economic depression returned in 1883-7. At any rate, we know that they joined a church near their home in Green Street. This congregation, in Stephenson Street, belonged to the United Presbyterian Church, another Calvinist denomination close in spirit to the Free Church of Scotland. Their first four children were all baptised there on the same Sunday in 1886, an event which might suggest a renewal of church-going after a lapse of some time. They remained in association with this church until at least 1894 when Margaret had her eighth child baptised there. She called him Thomas Irvine, which, despite a minor variation in spelling, might have been a mark of respect for the two outstanding preachers of evangelicalism associated with Calton, Thomas Chalmers and Edward Irving.

Chalmers and Irving were leading evangelical preachers in the 1840s who stimulated charitable endeavour among the poorest working class of the district, and the tradition remained strong right down to the childhood of Willie Patterson.

This is hardly surprising. Churches were still the only safety net for respectable working-class people when times were hard. Unemployed men had no entitlement to relief by the poor law boards, whose decisions were, in any case, greatly influenced by the ministers of religion who served on them. Looking back from the 1930s, an 'old Caltonian' doctor testified to the authority of Calton ministers in the 1880s. It was marked by outward and visible signs. The minister was a gentleman, going about the streets in frock coat, 'lum hat' and white tie. He needed no clerical collar to distinguish him, for doctors were the only other people who dressed like that in Calton, and the doctor himself was usually a church elder.

In conduct, one of the ministers seemed especially to exemplify the old community ways:

> *He placed the case of the poor before the richer members of his flock and acted as an almoner, always with discretion as well as sympathy. He got many a boy his start in life, and would walk miles to help a man to a job. And he said nothing about it. He had no newspaper or platform reputation, but ... after years of such work, he was known and blessed by many an old body who had outlived her friends and by many a young man who had had no chance of making a start in life but for him.*[17]

According to the same witness, there were many local shopkeepers and tradesmen among the congregations who plied their business in the new, improved streets. They shared in the ministers' sense of responsibility and assisted them in the task of distinguishing the deserving from the undeserving poor:

> *They knew their customers and were known by them ... Cash payments were the rule, and individual purchases mainly small, but they helped their customers to tide over bad times by giving them credit.*[18]

Unemployed men, he tells us, had to rely on the help of such sponsors:

> *Any odd job was welcomed, and many odd jobs turned up now and then.*[19]

* * * * * *

It is highly likely that Willie's father and mother had to depend on these ministers and churchgoers to eat the bread of charity during hard times in their early married life. Five more children followed Willie in the next ten years and the hardships of the family during the first

---

[17] Devon, *Calton Fifty Years Ago*, p. 34-5
[18] Devon, pp. 34-5

thirteen years of marriage are indicated by the fact that the home they occupied was a one-roomed dwelling. Given the infant mortality statistics, it seems a miracle that so many of the little Pattersons survived their early years.

Indeed family breakdown was common enough in these circumstances. The 'old Caltonian' doctor recalled that 'Some men were broken by their experiences and learnt to live by loafing. Most,' he added, 'kept their self-respect through it all.'

Joseph was one of the latter. Almost to the end of his life, he clung to his precarious status, just above the manual labourer and just below that of the small shopkeepers and clerks on the lowest ranks of middle class respectability. From the baptismal records of Calton United Presbyterian Church, we glean some knowledge of this struggle. Between 1883 and 1894, he changed occupation four times, rising from china packer to salesman, falling back to packer, then rising a little to the position of shop man, only to fall back again to packer. During this time, the growing family moved house three times, the first 'flit' taking them only to a two-roomed dwelling in Stevenson Street, near the church.[20] These moves between jobs in the glass and china trade and among the mean streets of Glasgow's East End could have brought little material improvement, but they show that the family held their position on the margin of respectability, just above the abyss of poverty. When Joseph was in work, at least the children would have had porridge for the breakfast table, vegetable broth and bread and cheese for dinner.

Willie never forgot Joseph's efforts to cling on to respectability. Indeed he seems to have come to hold an exaggerated impression of his father's status, for, in later life, the son represented his father as a 'china merchant'. This, at any rate, is how Willie's second wife entered Joseph's occupation on her husband's death certificate in 1953. Since she could not have known Joseph, who died of peritonitis in 1905, when he was in work as an engineer's machine man, it seems reasonable to believe that Willie gave her this flattering view of his father's trade. It was the act of a man who felt ashamed of

---

[19] Devon, p. 52

[20] Information supplied from census by Mitchell Library, Glasgow

his humble origins and perhaps also his misspent youth. Pride in his later achievements led him to colour up the background from which he emerged as a means of enhancing his dignity.

* * * * * *

Thus Willie grew to youth and early manhood in, we might surmise, an atmosphere of sobriety, industry and puritanism, attending church and Sunday School each week. A most pressing concern of his father and mother would have been to keep him out of trouble. Yet this was not easy in a place like Calton and in a large family. Joseph would have worked long hours and Margaret had her work cut out with the arrival of successive children. As they rose in years, the three older boys would have had a good deal of latitude to roam and play in the manner observed by Dr Russell.

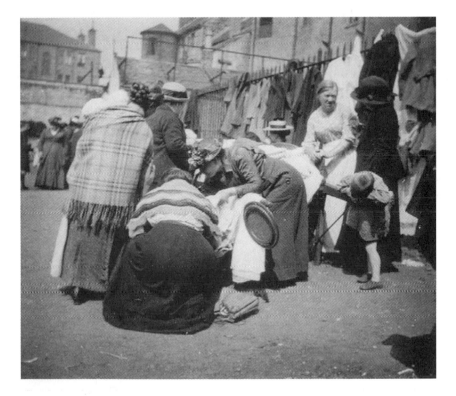

Women looking through clothes at the Barrows (Glasgow Museums)

Joseph and Margaret would certainly have worried about the corrupting distractions of the Calton streets. Scenes of drunkenness were everywhere – there were no fewer than ten public houses in and around Green Street which was approximately 300 yards long. At the northern end was the site of the local flea market, the 'Barrows'. It was the colourful haunt of dubious dealers in second-hand wares – a 'heterogeneous mass of clothing, clocks, watches, hats, umbrellas, parasols, rugs, metal, pictures, books, and other things too numerous to mention.'[21] It was also a fertile breeding ground for crime, a haunt of those who frequented the many shebeens, gambling dens and pubs of the district.

Not that Calton lacked its sunnier side. At the southern end of Green Street, lay Glasgow Green. This was the ancient common land of the City, dedicated to a variety of pastimes and usage. Sheep still grazed upon it when Willie was a boy. In mid-century, it had been laid out with fine monuments and pleasant walks which still offered some vistas of the Clyde and the green hills that overlooked it. But it is unlikely that Margaret Patterson entirely approved of it as a playground for her children. As the 'Speaker's Corner' of the City, it was often the scene of vigorous disputation on matters she would not have liked them to overhear. Orangemen fiercely denounced the Pope. Atheists attacked believers. Fiery radicals scorned the Government. Drunks argued with teetotallers. In short, cranks of every kind swarmed in abundance.

Clearly, there was much in Calton to seduce a growing boy and develop the wild side of his character. Willie's army record suggests that he was not indifferent to the temptations. This was not for lack of countervailing influences, and could even have been something of a reaction against them. Since 1751, when Samuel Wesley had preached from a stool on Glasgow Green, a long line of evangelicals, philanthropists and municipal improvers had been striving to civilise and sanitise 'the Calton' and its restless population. The tradition was still vigorous in Willie's youth and its exponents loved to point to the many provisions made in Calton to 'uplift the

---

[21] Fyfe, A tour in the Calton, p. 278

race'.[22] Handsome buildings survived from the past: famous eighteenth century churches, for example. In Charlotte Street, the house of the early nineteenth century cotton master and philanthropist, David Dale, was now occupied by the Salvation Army. There was a home for orphans, a school for poor boys, common lodging houses for men and women, and the celebrated Tent Hall where free breakfasts were served to the poor each Sunday, followed by evangelical preaching. More recently, municipal enterprise had built a public washhouse and baths. There was, too, an 'old clothes market' in Greendyke Street, its clean, airy premises provided by the Corporation as an alternative to flea pits like 'Paddy's Market', haunted by filthy rag pickers.

Tent Hall, Steel Street (Glasgow Museums)

---

[22] Fyfe, *A Tour in the Calton*, p. 267

Did Margaret try to steer her lads towards these improving institutions and away from the pubs and gambling dens? We do not know, but it is certain that Willie participated (albeit minimally) in another of the great Victorian 'improvements' introduced in 1872. In that year, the Education (Scotland) Act provided elementary education for all children. There was no comparable system of secondary education until 1918, and fees were not abolished until 1890, but many working-class boys benefited sufficiently from a solid grounding in 'the three Rs' to proceed to apprenticeships in skilled trades. A few, like Willie's near contemporary, the coal miner John Wheatley, did much better, proceeding through voluntary adult education to professional or political careers. But participation did not guarantee success and young Willie was far from successful, leaving elementary school with little to show for it. As we shall see, his subsequent education and training in the army suggests that he was insecure in the basic 'three Rs'.

Green Street Industrial School (Glasgow Museums)

He left school to work as an unskilled labourer. It was a common enough fate. Schooling of poor working-class children was often interrupted by illness and absenteeism. The older children of a working-class family, moreover, had little chance of early advancement. There was no extra money to pay for their indenture to a trade and their labour was often vital to augment the family income. 'Staying on' for secondary education was therefore rarely an option. Few children even managed to complete the official course of full time elementary education to age thirteen. They could change to half-time education at age ten. Few did so in Willie's day but, by the same token, few remained to thirteen.[23] Many boys, therefore, followed their fathers into years of toil in dead-end jobs for low wages, just as girls left to help their mothers at home.

Willie had not done as well as his father and there may have been an additional explanation for his relatively poor performance. In view of Willie's later display of male chauvinism, it is one that deserves some consideration. One effect of the Education Act had been to feminise the teaching profession. Young women[24] were recruited in substantial numbers to fill up the ranks of a service that was hard put to cope with the influx of additional students which the Act enforced. These young women, some of them trained in the church training colleges, were instructed to 'develop grace and gentleness in the children under their care.'[25] Students were not usually taught by male teachers until they reached the second last year of primary education. This meant that, for boys in Willie's station, there was a tension between classroom and street. The latter required boys to develop a tough, aggressive personality. The former worked the other way, often with threats of punishment by hell fire.[26] If, to this

---

[23] J Scotland, *The History of Scottish Education, II: from 1872 to the Present* (1969) p. 57

[24] Helen Corr, 'The Sexual Division of Labour in the Scottish Teaching Profession, 1872-1914', in W M Humes and H Paterson, *Scottish Culture and Scottish Education, 1880-1980* (Edinburgh, 1983) p. 138f

[25] Corr, 'The Sexual Division of Labour', in Humes and Paterson, *Scottish Culture and Scottish Education*, p. 142

[26] Scotland, *History of Scottish Education, II*, p. 51

was added the frustrations of an evangelical home life, a degree of alienation from school and church might be expected.

Nothing in the curriculum or regime of the average Scottish school of those days would have been likely to counteract this by stimulating his imagination. Classes were large – officially limited to seventy, but in practice as big as a hundred. Most of the day was given up to the 'three Rs' and subjects like history and geography were regarded as 'frills' by most Scottish teachers.[27] Children went to school for serious hard work and discipline was commonly enforced by corporal punishment with the 'tawse', a thick leather strap.

* * * * * *

The full significance of this early experience will emerge as Willie's story unfolds. We must now close this chapter by trying to imagine the frustrations of Willie Patterson's teenage years as an unskilled labourer in Glasgow. It was a city of marked contrasts. As Manny Shinwell, a poor Jewish boy from the East End and Willie's exact contemporary who became a Labour Cabinet Minister, put it: there were 'two Glasgows'. There were the wealth and glitter of fashionable Buchanan Street or Sauchiehall Street and the drab streets of the East end. Calton, grim enough in itself, was surrounded by decaying slums, deserted wastes and dingy industrial plants. To the south, across the river, lay Gorbals, once a fashionable suburb, now an industrial wasteland of coal mining and iron smelting. To the north, Calton shaded into the lower, and seedier end of Dennistoun, where stood the grim pile of Duke Street prison, ironically nicknamed the 'Eastern Hotel' by locals. This was 'the East End' which was 'closely built, and intersected in every direction by dark and filthy closes, the abodes of the poor, the wretched and the criminal.'[28]

Beyond Glasgow Cross, however, the glittering world of the West End beckoned. For Glasgow was still almost a walking city. If the economic gulf between riches and poverty was vast, the distance between the far end of Sauchiehall Street and Glasgow Cross was scarcely two miles. Young working men like Shinwell, on business

---

[27] Scotland, p. 50
[28] Scotland p. 136

errands for their employers, could saunter 'up Sauchie, doon Buchie and alang Argyle', taking in the enticing spectacle and mingling with the toffs. Watching how the other half lived, a lad might begin to wonder how he might escape from poverty and privation.

But how could Willie break out of his narrow, mean existence? It was a question which many young men were beginning to ask, even those more fortunately placed than he. Their discontent had its beginning in that break with Victorian evangelicalism which was so marked a feature of the 1890s, the decade in which Oscar Wilde flouted the conventions of bourgeois society and Bernard Shaw championed the cause of 'the devil's disciple'. They signalled the turn to a new century of cultural hedonism, an age of mass consumption and the pursuit of material pleasures. It was not just an affair of London and the metropolitan intelligentsia. Its early seismic movements were also felt by Glasgow youth.[29] In the West End, university students and young 'swells' hung out at risqué bars and restaurants. Working-class youth found its own scope for fun. To the west of Glasgow Cross, along the Gallowgate and Argyle Street, were many haunts of 'low' pleasure. Young Shinwell found sport and adventure in the boxing booths. Willie could have found excitement in the music halls that were opening everywhere, touting sensational shows in which female dancers with long legs were strutting the boards. Was this the origin of that sense of fun which Willie's daughter remembered from her childhood, just after the First World War? For a copper or two, he could have seen the shows which often celebrated Britain's expanding Empire and conquest of wild 'savages'.

If he did, it would have been in spite of the churches and the city improvers who waged war against music halls like the Britannia in nearby Trongate. For a century, evangelical city fathers had been striving to let Glasgow flourish 'by the preaching of the word' (as the motto on its coat of arms had it) – hence their endeavours in church building and charitable foundations. More lately, municipal reformers tried supplementing Scripture with 'culture'. When Templeton's new

---

[29] J Mangan and J Walvin (Eds.), *Manliness and Morality: Middle-Class Masculinity in Britain and America, 1800-1940* (Manchester, 1987)

carpet factory opened on Glasgow Green, the Corporation decreed that it must be designed in a lofty style, so it was modelled on the Doge's Palace at Venice. A decade later a 'People's Palace' was added, to provide art and good music for the deprived denizens of the East End.

Templeton's Factory (Glasgow Museums)

Music for the ear, architecture for the eye – these were the means by which the middle classes sought to soothe the savage breast in Calton. But neither the wonders of the People's Palace nor the remarkable architecture of Templeton's factory could fire the imagination of young men like Willie. They wanted physical, not just imaginary escape from the East End. Remaining at home to repeat father's experience presented no attractions. Early marriage, a 'pickle o' weans' in an overcrowded tenement 'hoose', rearing them on a labourer's wage, constantly threatened by unemployment, was no life for a spirited young man. In any case, what security could Scotland offer at a time when there was no system of unemployment benefit, no child allowances from the state and no pensions to provide even a pittance in old age? Socialists were beginning to agitate for such things at open-air pitches on Glasgow Green, but Willie's background was not one that encouraged such thinking. A stay-at-home future must therefore have seemed as drab and uninviting as the closes, alleys and streets of the East End itself. But how to escape? There were not many ways out for youths like him. We have seen that the educational route was closed; likewise apprenticeship. Another possible way out was emigration. Around two million emigrants left the shores of Scotland between 1871 and 1914 to seek their fortunes in the United States or the British colonies. Emigration, however, usually required some resources, a bit saved up for the passage money and often kin or friends to provide the newcomer with some support on foreign soil. No evidence suggests that Willie was in such a position.

If apprenticeship and emigration were barred to Willie, only one other Victorian institution seemed to offer easy escape – the army. At almost any other time in the nineteenth century, such a leap would have been considered very shocking in evangelical circles. We have seen how Ulster Presbyterians objected to military exercises and martial music on Sundays. To respectable people in the nineteenth century, soldiers were considered as the lowest of the low, the outcasts and dregs of industrial society, who went as fighting men because they were fit for nothing else. But things were rather different now. From the 1870s, new industrial powers like Germany, Russia and France were challenging Britain's worldwide supremacy. By the 1890s, war clouds were gathering over Africa. A 'New Imperialism' took root in the consciousness of many British writers, statesmen and publicists. A new climate of militarism formed, not least in the West of Scotland.

Evangelicalism was not unaffected for it had its own militaristic and imperialistic tendencies. Anti-slavery and missionary endeavour led it to celebrate a new type of godly soldier, exemplified by General Charles Gordon, whose death at Khartoum in 1885 had elevated him to the status of a Christian martyr. In this climate of 'New Imperialism', many working-class boys turned away from the captains of industry towards the recruiting sergeants of the army. Willie Patterson was one of them.

The People's Palace on the Green. *The Baillie* **1897** (Glasgow Museums)

Chapter Three

Calton and the Nile

'With a people prosperous, contented, manly, intelligent and self-reliant, we may look forward with great hope.'[30]

From one point of view, there was nothing new in the 'New Imperialism' of late nineteenth century Britain. The British Empire had been expanding in India, Africa and Australasia for decades before Gladstone occupied Egypt in 1882. But from another point of view, there was a 'New Imperialism' in the sense that politicians and newspaper editors talked and wrote as if there was one. Willie developed to manhood in this cultural context and it stained his later personality indelibly.

Enthusiasts for Empire were reacting to events on a European, even a global scale. For one thing, the United States, vastly strengthened after the civil war of the 1860s, emerged as a rival to British influence and power in South America and the Caribbean. Later, in 1870, Bismarck unified Germany and proclaimed the King of Prussia its 'Kaiser' or 'Emperor'. Later still, in 1876/77, the Russian Empire went to war against the Ottoman Empire in Turkey. This seemed to threaten the Suez Canal and India, as did Russian attempts to secure influence over Afghanistan. The British Conservative leader, Benjamin Disraeli, responded to these alarms with a wake-up call to John Bull. In his widely noted Crystal Palace speech of 1872, he challenged British youth to seek careers and adventure in the colonies and, in 1876, proclaimed Queen Victoria 'Empress of India'. In 1876/7 he threatened war if Russia should occupy Constantinople, and

---

[30] Extract from *The Times* editorial of 1 January 1901

ended his government in 1879 by pushing British arms into Afghanistan.

Though William Gladstone, the Liberal leader, fiercely attacked this 'forward' policy in his election campaign of 1880, he was himself soon adding red to the map by occupying Egypt to secure the Suez Canal. Thus was set off a train of events that was to partition Africa, at first by drawing lines on maps, and later, as Willie was growing up, by military conquest in which Britain played its part by invading Sudan and annexing the Boer Republics in South Africa. In this chapter, we shall see how these great events affected one obscure lad growing up in Calton.

* * * * * *

Egypt could not be held and administered without its annual gift of floodwater from the River Nile. From the mid 1880s, successive British governments dreaded the occupation of countries lying to the south, such as Sudan and Abyssinia, by hostile European rivals, who might then, by some means or other, dam the Nile and deny irrigation to Egyptian fields. From this paranoia stemmed a series of bloody and menacing events.

In 1885, the British General Gordon and his small force were annihilated at Khartoum, vainly attempting to prevent Sudan from falling under the power of the Mahdi, a local Islamic leader. In the next few years, Britain spent much diplomatic effort in the 'scramble for Africa', trying to shut the back door to the Nile. But from the mid-nineties, these tensions broke into military action that threatened to embroil Britain with her colonial rivals.

In 1896, Britain watched while Abyssinia crushed Italian colonial aggression at the battle of Adowa. London was alarmed, not at the defeat of Italy, but at the military support given to Abyssinia by France, intensely jealous of a British Egypt. It seemed possible that Abyssinian power would spread northward into Sudan at Egypt's back door. London believed that this was the aim of French policy. Under Lord Salisbury's Conservative government, Britain decided to invade the Sudan and frustrate French plans. An army under Kitchener defeated the Sudanese at the battle of Omdurman in 1898. The slaughter of 11,000 Sudanese by British firepower did not immediately resolve the crisis, for France had dispatched a military expedition under Marchand to the head waters of the Nile. Marchand's orders were to look for a suitable site for the construction of a dam. To counter this, London ordered Kitchener to advance with his force up the Nile and confront Marchand at Fashoda. Faced by this military challenge, France backed down and was henceforth shut out of the Nile Valley.

Behind these wars and threats of war stood India, 'The Jewel in the Crown' of Britain's Empire. Governed as a Crown Colony since the Mutiny of 1857, she constituted a vast market for English cotton goods and a valuable source of tea and other tropical foods. Indian troops fought for Britain in her colonial wars and Britain's trade surplus with India largely offset her growing deficit with industrial rivals like the United States.

* * * * * *

This was the structure of imperial power that was to influence Willie's life, both for good and ill. During his boyhood and youth, India was never far from British consciousness. In 1887 the Queen celebrated her Golden Jubilee in London. In the following year, an International Exhibition of Science and Art was held in Glasgow. Kelvingrove Museum was used to display the presents which the queen had received from the loyal subjects of her Indian Empire. A new tearoom was built in Kelvingrove Park after the style of an Anglo-Indian bungalow. Military power was much on display. At the opening of the exhibition, the Prince and Princess of Wales reviewed over 10,000 troops. The Queen herself visited the exhibition twice. It is possible that the Pattersons were among the five million other visitors, for evangelically-minded people warmed to the habits of temperance signified by the exotic tearoom.

Willie was only four years of age at that time, but the exhibition left a lasting memorial much nearer home. The Doulton Drinking Fountain had been made for the Exhibition and was moved from Kelvingrove Park to Glasgow Green in 1890. It was the gift, appropriately enough, of a china manufacturer. Surmounted by the figure of Queen Victoria, the peoples of the Empire were represented as life-size male and female figures.

In the ensuing years, Empire and militarism entered into the consciousness of Scottish people at many levels. For example, 'the institutions of British government and the Empire' was a compulsory subject in schools under the 1872 Act. So was 'military drill. When Willie was fourteen, the nation celebrated the Queen's Diamond Jubilee. This was a far more glittering and imperialistic affair than her golden jubilee had been.

In this triumphalist atmosphere, militarism began to strike deeper roots among those sections of the British working class which had hitherto despised soldiering. Indeed, it was just around the time of Willie's birth that Empire, militarism and Christianity were being fused into a heady brew by the formation of uniformed youth organisations and by the recruiting campaigns of the British army. In the eyes of some evangelical Christians, military discipline came to be seen as a character forming panacea for the social evil of 'hooliganism' – the rowdy, brawling, drunken conduct of the city streets. The Boys Brigade, for example, was set up in Glasgow in 1883 to instil military discipline in working-class youths who had alarmed slum missionaries and Sunday School teachers by their rowdiness and insubordination.[31] The BB targeted the East End with the notion that manly submission to discipline was the hallmark of a Christian youth. Part-time service in the militia was encouraged by the BB and pushed by employers who linked Imperial defence with trade.

In the last chapter, we noted how the feminisation of the teaching profession progressed during these years, tending to produce resentment among their male colleagues and also perhaps among the boys they taught. 'Masculinity' became a more conscious life-style choice for youth in these years. Imperialism and militarism fostered the sense that boys must grow up tough and hardy defenders of the British race. It will be important to remember this cultural change when we come to consider Willie's unhappy marriage. The cult of manliness was gradually being altered and spread from the public

---

[31] Mangan and Walvin (Eds), *Manliness and Morality*, p. 54 f.

schools to the lower working class. The reformed public schools of the nineteenth century had patronised woman as a lovely, but vulnerable creature, best fitted for the trials of domestic life. With the rise of Imperialism and militarism, this sense of gender difference was heightened and further exaggerated. Working-class youths were exhorted to reject all trace of 'effeminacy' from their personalities and to cultivate the manly qualities on which the security of the Empire must depend. In 1891, for example, William Alexander Smith, founder of the Boys Brigade, told an audience:

> *There is undoubtedly among boys an impression that to be a Christian means to be a 'mollycoddle' and in order to disabuse their minds of this idea we sought to construct our organisation on a model which would appeal to all their sentiments of manliness and honour.*[32]

These reformers detested the anarchistic violence of the slums which was often directed at them. They aimed to channel it into the controlled and disciplined violence of organised military force which, like General Gordon (a patron of the Boys Brigade), they wished to deploy in the service of Christian civilisation as they understood it. This was the attitude of one of the Vice-Presidents of the Boys Brigade, George Alfred Henty. Henty was the author of popular fiction for boys. He saw himself as instilling a spirit of manliness, steadfastness and courage in his young readers.[33] Henty's fiction held up for admiration public school heroes engaged in deeds of high Imperial adventure.

It might seem, at first sight, that this kind of reading was well beyond the reach of a lad like Willie Patterson. Yet it was certainly to be found in Calton during his boyhood, as the 'Old Caltonian' doctor, whose memoirs have figured prominently in the preceding pages, testified. He read surreptitiously '*Boys of England* and such forbidden stuff', borrowing them from a local circulating library. By contrast, his former taste for Maryatt, Fenimore Cooper, etc. seemed 'tame'.

---

[32] Mangan and Walvin, p. 55
[33] Mangan and Walvin, p. 61

Such fictions could appeal powerfully to boys like Willie, occupying a border position on the frontier between the ethnic communities of Ireland and Britain. Growing up in one of the roughest parts of nineteenth century Glasgow, surrounded by the drunkenness, brawling and whoring that was characteristic of such districts, he had to be ready with his fists and was influenced by values the very opposite of the evangelical sobriety of his parents. It would be surprising if he did not feel some conflict of loyalties. Was he to identify with the evangelical values of his family background, or should he revel in the life of the streets, with its adventurous experiments in booze, sex and fisticuffs?

And it was precisely this conflict to which the BB offered a new kind of resolution. A young man could sublimate aggression into disciplined combat for Christian civilisation, which it was the British Empire's historic destiny to uphold and extend. Frustratingly, we do not know whether Willie was a member of the Boys Brigade or not. It is tempting to assume that he was, for the BB in Glasgow seems to have been quite successful at attracting youth from the unskilled working class.[34]

Boys Brigade or not, there was one institution with similar aims which Willie did join: the militia. This auxiliary arm of part-time soldiers drew its main support from the unskilled working class. Recruits signed up for six years and undertook to drill with their companies on twenty-eight days in each year.

Willie enrolled in December 1900, at the age of seventeen. The most available militia company was attached to the Highland Light Infantry, a famous Scottish regiment whose barracks were then in Calton. Entry to this regiment suggests a strong assertion of 'British' identity on Willie's part, combined, perhaps, with a romantic sense of the Scottish past that was being fostered in the new music halls.

The militia also offered more tangible attractions. Employers were gratified – and rewarded – when their young employees volunteered. The boys got pay and uniform for annual drill. The

---

[34] Mangan and Walvin, p. 58

masculine camaraderie of camp life appealed strongly to any young men bored with industrial labour or exasperated by parental discipline and family rows. All this powerfully reinforced the popular culture purveyed by newspapers and music halls, by juvenile literature like Henty's novels or the 'penny dreadfuls'. It filled their heads with fantasies of escape, adventure and thrills in foreign lands.

* * * * * *

In the last year of the nineteenth century, the message was reinforced by the opening battles of the Boer War. Thousands of militia reservists served in the war and others undertook garrison duties on home stations to release regular troops. How did the Boer War come about and what was young Willie's attitude towards it?

It was the climax of a long struggle between rival European settlers for control of southern Africa, especially Transvaal, which was rich in gold and other minerals. Britain was determined that Transvaal should acknowledge her supremacy. The more ardent Imperialists, like the Colonial Secretary, Joseph Chamberlain, wanted a close association between the two Boer republics, Transvaal and Orange Free State, and the two British colonies of The Cape and Natal. The Afrikaners or Boers, descendants of the first Dutch settlers, were equally determined to frustrate his aims. 'Pro-Boers' in Britain liked to think of them as peasant farmers, nobly struggling for land and liberty against mighty mining companies and British Proconsuls. In reality, they were led by a rancher aristocracy who grudged sharing their liberty with anyone else – neither the white 'Uitlanders' who had emigrated to Transvaal during the gold rush, nor the black Africans, whom they treated as an inferior creation, divinely appointed to serve Dutch masters. The British demanded civil rights for the Uitlanders, but considered black Africans a childlike race destined to be 'civilised' under British protection. Either way, it meant that blacks would be exploited by Europeans for a very long time.

In 1899, the Boers broke off negotiations and attacked the Cape and Natal, besieging Kimberley, Ladysmith and Mafeking. The British found it hard to resist them effectively. Since the Crimean War in mid-century, they had faced only 'native' armies in the colonies.

They were unprepared for the kind of warfare waged by the Boers who defended their positions from well-dug trenches with rapid rifle fire and heavy artillery. British generals were slow to learn the ways of this modern warfare. They squandered men and resources on set-piece attacks which the Boers countered with devastating fire power. The British sent in a new Commander-in-Chief, Field Marshall Roberts, and reinforced the army in overwhelming numbers, driving the Boers back into their homelands. By June 1900, when Roberts had occupied the Boer capitals of Bloemfontein and Pretoria, it seemed that the war was practically over.

The British at home rapturously celebrated the relief of Ladysmith and Mafeking. In Glasgow a noisy crowd gathered outside a 'Pro-Boer' meeting. According to one eyewitness, 'flabby well-groomed medical students and dirty corner boys … bawled and sang and shouted' abuse at anyone thought to be on the unpatriotic side.[35] The Press revelled in the exploits of our gallant highlanders and the aged Queen Victoria visited Ireland to express her gratitude to her 'brave Irish'. In the 'Khaki election' of 1900, every constituency in Glasgow was won by the Conservative government which had taken Britain to war with the Boers. But the war dragged on for two more years. The Afrikaner farmers of the Veld took to guerrilla warfare on horseback, a tactic of which they proved masters. They harried the British lines of communication mercilessly. The British retaliated with 'methods of barbarism', burning Boer women and children out of their farms, detaining them in 'concentration camps' where thousands died of fever, and all the time driving the Boer commandos as British 'sportsmen' drove pheasants. Superior forces and vicious counter-guerrilla tactics slowly ground down Boer resistance until they sued for peace which was made at Vereeniging in May 1902, but not before British opinion had been sharply polarised between supporters and critics of the conduct of the war.

* * * * * *

The Boer War stirred up deep emotions in British youth who formed the Jingo mobs and hounded 'Pro-Boers'. Many were university

---

[35] *Glasgow Evening News*, 9 March 1900

students. Others came from the ranks of the 'black coated workers' – clerks – insecure and desperate to establish themselves. Still others, like Willie himself, were drawn from the unskilled working class who had suffered from the recent economic crises. All felt that the times were out of joint and some wanted to do their bit in putting them to rights. They resented the spectacle of a great power like Britain being pushed around by Lilliputian opponents like the Boers. They waxed indignant over the alleged 'decline of manliness', and resented the 'new woman' who was making her way into male preserves like the commercial office and the medical profession.

There is no direct evidence to tell us whether any of these influences moved Willie Patterson to join the regular army, but a clue is afforded by the date on which he chose to do so. He transferred from the militia in October 1902, on his nineteenth birthday, and six months after the peace of Vereeniging. The date shows that he could not have been eager for service in South Africa, for he would have been eligible for regular service on his eighteenth birthday in the previous year. His 'attestation', which all recruits had to make, survives today in the archive of the Ministry of Defence, but it is silent, unfortunately, on his motives for enlisting. Military bureaucracy, so punctilious over height, weight, colour of eyes etc., was completely indifferent to the motives of its recruits. For decades it had sought them among the unskilled working class who joined up to escape unemployment, domestic difficulties or the boredom of wage labour. Unemployment rose steadily during the war and it has been argued that working men enlisted out of economic need, having resisted the call of country in its early years. Such evidence as we have suggests that Willie enlisted out of a mixture of motives. It probably included a desire for economic opportunities that Glasgow could not afford, the adventure of military service, and a British patriotism that stopped short of death or glory in South Africa.

Certainly, unemployment was not his problem. His attestation shows he was in work at the time of enlistment. It also tells us that he had never been apprenticed to a trade. Like many other recruits, he worked as a labourer at around about a pound a week. Army pay, at sixpence a day, probably afforded as much disposable income as a labourer's wage, for the army provided clothing, rations and lodgings free of charge. It also afforded security for, in peacetime, there was less chance of being injured or killed in the army than in many working-class occupations.

Patriotic pride is a more complex matter. It was only slowly that immigrants like the Pattersons learnt to feel British. Men like Clark Patterson often looked back nostalgically, not to 'Ireland' as such, but to the locality from which they sprang, contrasting an idealised rural world with the grim conditions of mainland industrial cities. Neither Britishness nor Irishness had much appeal to them. Ireland was the land that had ejected them: Britain the land of their exile. The following ode to Kilrea, written by a Glasgow East Ender and near contemporary of Willie's grandfather, illustrates this intense local nostalgia for the very village of Clark's origin:

> Kilrea! Fairest spot on the face of the earth
> In this moment of backward reflection,
> Although thou'st denied me the place of my birth,
> Yet I love thee with tender affection.
> When I think of the past that's so quickly gone by,
> My breast heaves with heartfelt emotion,
> Sweet memories of old bring a tear to my eye –
> The tear of an honest devotion.
> How oft I have strolled by the banks of the Bann
> When the flushed summer sun was declining,
> Or leisurely rambled through sweet Moneygran
> 'Mid the woodbine and ivy entwining.
> Where the surface of 'Kathleen's' silvery shines
> In the shade of the Manor plantation,
> And the fields undulating in endless lines –
> What a beautiful work of creation.
> I have toiled in the fields and enjoyed my reward,
> For when all my labours were over
> I could lay myself down on the emerald sward
> 'Mid the perfume of daisies and clover.
> I've heard the birds chirrup their twittering note
> With a heart gay and light as a feather,
> I've seen the lark soar with a song in its throat,

From its haunt in Drumimerick heather.
Then long may this village by heaven designed
Adorn the fair county of Derry;
May prosperity, virtue and honour combined
Make the hearts of thy citizens merry.
They may sing of Killarney, Tralee and Kildare,
Other bards other places have chosen;
But wherever I roam I emphatically swear
Thy name shall repose in my bosom.[36]

But as the generations succeeded one another, this kind of sentiment declined. There were good reasons for the Pattersons to play down their Irish background in Calton. The 'Old Caltonian' doctor recalled:

The Irish were looked upon as an inferior race, hewers of wood and drawers of water, who should be treated with consideration but kept in their place. The less we had to do with them the better.[37]

Distrust of 'Paddies' was strongest, of course, towards Roman Catholics, but Ulster Protestants could also feel the coldness of Glaswegian Protestants who neglected to discriminate between Irish accents.

To counter social exclusion, some Irish emphasised their British Loyalties by joining the Orange Order.[38] As we have seen, the Pattersons did not go to such extremes. Yet they had every reason to counter the shifting instability of their lives and the hostility towards

---

[36] Quoted in Kilrea Local History Group, *The Fairy Thorn: Gleanings and Glimpses of Old Kilrea* (Kilrea, 1984) p. 153. (By permission of Kilrea Local History Group)

[37] *The Fairy Thorn*, p.31

[38] L Greenslade, 'White skin, white masks: psychological distress among the Irish in Britain' in P O'Sullivan (Ed), *The Irish in the New Communities* (Leicester, 1992) pp. 201-225. Greenslade shows that mental illness and alcoholism were higher than the British average among Irish immigrants in the 1970s. There is much evidence to show that this was also true in the mid-nineteenth century, though care should be taken to avoid attributing the response of a fraction to Irish immigrants as a whole. Cp. D Fitzpatrick, 'A peculiar tramping people: the Irish in Britain, 1801-70' in WE Vaughan (Ed), *Ireland under the Union* (Oxford, 1989), *Volume I* of *A New History of Ireland* ed. FX Martin et al, pp. 623-57

their kind by assimilating to the 'North Britishness' that was everywhere proclaimed in those days by the names of railways, newspapers and hotels.

This sense of British identity was fostered in the atmosphere that prevailed in the first year of the Boer War. Many felt the call of Queen and country. Some of these who have left us recollections of the time are interesting here because, like Willie, they belonged to marginal groups who needed to demonstrate their Britishness by patriotic sentiments and deeds. One was Manny Shinwell, the Labour politician and Willie's exact contemporary. He was a third generation descendant of poor Jewish immigrants who recalled, near the end of his life, that his patriotism was aroused by seeing the soldiers march to the docks through the Glasgow streets. He felt very patriotic and sided with Irish Unionists against nationalists when he overheard their arguments in his father's low class tailoring shop.

Another near contemporary was Frank Richards who published his memoirs under the title of the *Old Soldier Sahib*. Richards enlisted about the same time as Willie. As a youth, he had worked for low wages, first in the unhealthy conditions of a Welsh tin works and then as a miner. Underground, he met an old soldier who was always talking of his adventures in India which he described as 'a land of milk and honey'. The Boer War aroused patriotic British sentiment in this 'Taffy' so that he joined the Royal Welsh Fusiliers. In this atmosphere, it would be surprising if Willie did not feel patriotic sentiment swelling in his own heart.

In passing, we may wonder how his parents reacted. 'Going for a soldier' sometimes provoked, or sprang from, domestic quarrels. There is no hint of family friction at Calton. Evangelicalism and militarism were often close bedfellows and Willie was still living in the family home (which had been moved yet again to Baltic Street in Bridgeton) when he joined the army in 1902. The fact that he would one day call his own son Joseph, after his father, and his second daughter Margaret, after his mother, may suggest that he honoured his father and mother and that they approved (or at least did not oppose) his break with industry and sobriety to seek his fortune in the field of war.

* * * * * *

From the militia Willie would have expected to pass into the regular army regiment of the Highland Light Infantry. The regiment linked civic pride and British patriotism. Glasgow boasted itself 'the second city of the Empire' and the HLI linked the martial traditions of the Highland clans, the flourishing industry of the Clyde and the expansion of 'greater Britain' in a heady brew of identity with a great force in the world. Towards the end of the Boer War, however, recruiting for the HLI was closed and Willie's natural progression into the regiment was blocked. He turned instead to an Irish regiment, The Connaught Rangers.

The switch is suggestive of Willie's sense of identity at this time. He was aligning himself, not with the land of his forefathers, but with the British Empire. Such behaviour was characteristic of many Protestant 'Paddies', who emphasised their loyalty to Britain as a compensation for the hostility of their English or Scottish hosts. Irish regiments of the British army were really a colonial garrison force, intended to support the police in suppressing rebellious behaviour by the natives. Officered, in the main, by British gentlemen, the other ranks were predominantly English and Scottish. Barracks, constructed like the forts of an occupying power, were intended for the suppression of nationalistic uprisings. The Connaught Rangers' barracks at Galway was set on the coast of a province in which the poor Catholic peasantry had been militant for repeal of the union with Britain. The regiment thus existed to overawe the Irish with foreign force, but it also helped to counter dissidence by recruiting some of its strength from that same peasantry, and thereby harnessing the fighting traditions of the Irish to the Unionist cause. All recruits were schooled in this sentiment by the regimental symbols of Union. Their cap badge displayed a harp surmounted by a crown representing Irish loyalty to the British state. 'Who will separate them?' asked its motto. The Rangers had been in the thick of the early battles against the Boers and earned great public praise with the rest of the Irish Brigade. In the last phase of the war, its mounted infantry played a conspicuous part in driving the Boer commandos across the rivers and mountains of the Veld, and the British press set even their blunders in a heroic light.

All in all, then, Willie's approach to army service was probably like that of many young men without education or skill in the Scottish working class. The military offered adventure, a masculine ethos, economic security and an escape from the confinement of narrow opportunities. No doubt the climate of 'New Imperialism' had stimulated his patriotism and the army offered a strong sense of Britishness at a time when Scottish and Irish identities were weak and suspect. Deprived of enrolment in a Glasgow regiment, Willie went beyond local pride and reconstructed the Irish traditions of his forebears. He cast aside their devotion to industry, sobriety and evangelicalism and slipped into Irish regimentals. Yet time would show that this was not a fundamental break. The late Victorian army offered opportunity to develop the spirit of self-help displayed by Clark and Joseph Patterson. That spirit had driven his grandfather to leave Ireland. It had moved his father's restless quest for self-improvement. Now it was moving Willie to escape the mean streets around Glasgow Green. Not for him the People's Palace and the Winter Gardens – nor yet the desperate glory of war. What exactly he would find in the service of King and country was probably not entirely clear, but he would seek that fortune, whatever it might be, in a wider, more colourful world than Calton could offer.

Chapter Four

India

'It is useless to pretend that our life was a normal one. Ours was a one-sexed society, with the women hanging on to the edges. In India there was always an unnatural tension ... and every man who pursued the physical aim of sexual relief was in danger of developing a cynical hardness and lack of sympathy ... '[39]

When Willie presented himself at Hamilton Barracks, Sergeant Wilmington looked him over with a practised eye and noted down the features that interested the military. They were not over impressive. At five feet four and a quarter he was barely an inch above the minimum height for recruitment, and his weight was only 116 lbs.

This was a matter of general concern. The army had had to reject, as unfit for military service, almost half the recruits who presented themselves during the Boer War. Parliamentary investigations suggested that there had been an alarming 'physical deterioration' of the working-class population during the nineteenth century. The average height of a well-developed lad of eighteen was officially estimated at five feet seven inches, with a weight of 137 lbs. In the light of this, Willie's physique could only be described by the recruiting sergeant as 'fair'. His saving grace, however, was the absence of any deformities, marks or signs of previous illness, such as the bow-legs that betrayed childhood rickets. Here was a basically healthy physique which the drill instructor could make something of: no need to reject this man as a sweeping from the Glasgow slums.

---

[39] John Masters on military service in India in the 1930s, quoted in R Hyam, *Empire and Sexuality: The British Experience* (Manchester, 1992) p. 122

As to his general appearance at this time, the medical inspection notes give only a few hints. It was noted that his hair was light brown and his eyes grey but, since these features were recorded on later army records as 'fair' and 'blue' respectively, it seems safe to say that his hair was on the darker side of fair – what Glaswegians call 'moosie broon' – and he possessed the clear blue eyes inherited by most of his descendants.

Almost immediately on recruitment, Willie was transferred to Renmore Barracks, Galway, the depot or home base of the Connaught Rangers. What he found there was a microcosm of the class system that divided officers from 'other ranks' in the British army. A walled-in square, some 800 yards by 800 yards, was home to about a thousand human beings and a considerable number of transport horses. The men slept in rooms arranged in 'lines' along the northern side. Up to a hundred rankers were crammed into rooms about thirty feet by fifteen, sleeping in bunks which rose up to three tiers. In emergencies such as war, additional men were housed under canvas in the field behind the fortifications. The married quarters, situated on the opposite side from the 'lines', were equally cramped, each family occupying just one room in the long building.

The Socialist editor, Robert Blatchford, set down in 1910 recollections of his own life in army barracks, some twenty to thirty years earlier. As a naïve young chapel-goer from Yorkshire who had taken the Queen's shilling during a spell of unemployment, he was at first shocked and repelled at the levity of many men. There was always a lot of drinking. Men would fight over possession of a French newspaper with 'disgusting pictures'[40] and their language made him 'physically sick'[41] The truth is that army barracks were slums, inhabited by men, young and old, many of whom had come from slums. It was little better in Willie's day than it had been in Blatchford's, just as the 1950s scenes of National Service depicted in David Lodge's novel *Ginger You're Balmy* were little improved from Willie's time.

---

[40] R Blatchford, *My Life in the Army* (London, 1910) p. 23
[41] R Blatchford, p. 6

Officers, therefore, kept their distance from the men and the marks of this class system can still be seen today in Renmore, now in the Irish Republic. In Willie's day, there were four messes: three facing the 'lines', one for privates, a second for corporals and a third for sergeants. Today the messes for Irish NCOs are combined, but the fourth – the officers' mess – still stands apart, palm trees at the door, recalling the Indian army where so many Rangers served. A neat lawn, fronting the ornate facade, was in Willie's time a tennis court, exclusively devoted to the relaxation of those who held the King's Commission. Such were the privileges of class which seemed necessary in that confined space, where a gentleman's disgust at the physical proximity of working-class men had to be compensated by psychological distance.

Renmore Barracks, 1958 – little changed since Willie's time (Renmore Barracks)

Recruits were required to sign up for at least three years with the colours and another nine years in the reserve, but Willie eschewed this 'short service' option and volunteered 'to complete eight years with the colours'. Here we have another clue to his motives in joining the army. Since very few soldiers extended their service in this way, we may assume that army life was agreeable to him and, indeed, as Frank Richards' memoirs suggest, service life could be rewarding for a spirited young man living away from home for the first time. Like the young Welshman, Willie would have enjoyed the comradeship of the barracks, drinking in the 'wet canteen' and walking out in his best uniform. Perhaps, like Richards, he soon lost his virginity, for he seems to have been a rather wild young man. At any rate, during his initial training at Finner Camp, he was twice placed on a charge – first for drunkenness and disorderly conduct in the street, and next for leaving fatigue without permission and swearing at an NCO. Later, when he was transferred from training camp to Ship Street Barracks, Dublin, he again fell foul of the regimental authorities, this time for breaking out of barracks and remaining absent without leave.

Such charges were commonplace in army life and minor offences were sometimes overlooked if the sergeant happened to be in a good mood. But army discipline was intended to be harsh. Seven days confined to barracks, with its rounds of exhausting drill under the lash of the NCO's tongue, soon repressed the spirit of rebellion. Most men learned to 'play the old soldier' and accept normal duties as preferable to punishment. The aim of the army was to instil discipline and unquestioning obedience into its raw recruits. They must learn to stand firm in battle, to handle their arms with speed and deadly accuracy and, above all, to obey orders without question or hesitation. This was the point of the daily drill which a soldier in training had to undergo. Though boring enough, they were not without their compensations. Regular parades on the barrack square, begun immediately after reveille at dawn, continued at intervals until almost dusk. At night there were often guard and picket duties to perform. Route marches, carrying more than 70 lbs of kit over fifteen miles a day, improved the physique of the recruit. Willie was more than an inch taller when he left the army and his chest measurement had increased by two inches.

Other duties, though boring, instilled habits of personal responsibility. Buttons and straps had to be kept gleaming with Brasso and pipe clay. The men cared for their own quarters, scrubbing out mess and barrack rooms daily.

There were financial compensations too. Pay, at over a shilling a day, was certainly not princely, but it was at least regular. On top of it, the army provided a 'best uniform' and working fatigues, together with lodgings and rations. The latter consisted of a daily allowance of three-quarters of a pound of meat, a pound of bread, vegetables, tea and sugar. When supplies of wholesome food were available and corruption kept down to a minimum, these were better than a civilian diet for unskilled workingmen. There were extras like butter and eggs which could be purchased out of army pay. In a masculine sphere like the army, moreover, arrangements mirrored the division of labour between the sexes back home, for the wives of older soldiers did laundry for the younger men at a small charge.

Soldiers grumbled of course – about the deductions from their pay, about the quality and quantity of the rations, which were by no means always up to official standard, and about uncomfortable quarters – but many warmed to the *esprit de corps* of their regiment, which was said to be exceptionally strong in the Connaught Rangers. Traditional songs, said to have been sung at every concert in barracks, enhanced their self-esteem as the fiercest fighters and fastest lovers in the British army:

> *You may talk about your Guards, boys,*
> *Your Lancers and Hussars, boys,*
> *Your Fusiliers and Royal Artillery without the guns!*
> *The girls we drive them crazy,*
> *The foe we bate them aisy,*
> *The Rangers from Ould Connaught the land beyond the Sea!*[42]

Pride in the regiment was also nurtured by schooling men in its history. Battle honours were inscribed on the colours which were

---

[42] H F N Jourdain, *Ranging Memories* (1934) p. 50. Reprinted by permission of Oxford University Press

paraded before the assembled men on the anniversary of each glorious action, when an account of the affair would be read aloud to them. One of the quainter customs, in which Willie would have participated, was that of marching behind 'Jingling Johnny', a Moorish musical instrument which had been captured from the French at the battle of Salamanca in 1812. The original trophy was now treasured in the mess, but a replica was always carried at the front of parades and the tallest man in the Connaught Rangers had the honour of bearing it.

The importance of such rituals should not be under-estimated. They supported the regimental system which some military historians have seen, at least in retrospect, as the lynch pin of the British army. The new recruit found a home and a family in his regiment. It became a focus of identity and pride, constraining him to a code of conduct and a cause worth dying for.

This is probably not wholly fanciful, but the ironic view of the rank-and-file is equally well caught in *A Soldier's Catechism* which was reproduced in the memoirs of Lt Colonel H F N Jourdain, an officer of the Connaught Rangers in Willie's time:

> *Question: What is your name?*
> *Answer: A soldier.*
> *Question: Who gave you that name?*
> *Answer: The recruiting sergeant when he gave me the enlisting shilling, whereby I became an inheritor of the sword, bullet, and death.*
> *Question: What did the recruiting sergeant then promise you?*
> *Answer: He promised and vowed a good many things in my name, but these are the things he did not promise me: 1. That I must renounce all idea of liberty or any expectation of fair play. 2. That I should be put on short pay and well humbugged with any amount of drill. 3. That I should stand to be shot at whenever required for so trifling a matter.*
> *Question: Do you verily believe that you are bound to do these things?*

Answer: Yes, verily, and by the help of John Barleycorn or any of his prescriptions I hope when my services are required that I shall not be late or absent.[43]

In Willie's case, this self-mocking irony eventually turned into a sense of grievance and injustice and, as we shall see, he was to fall out with the Connaught Rangers.

We should also remember that *esprit de corps* had its negative side. Soldiers of one regiment often hated the men of another on account of some real or imagined insult or injury done to their comrades in former times. Especially when drink was flowing, tribal antagonisms could be stirred up by a jibe or taunt. On such occasions, fights broke out and each side confronted the other, like rival gangs. Cursing men threw punches, swung belts and kicked out with heavily booted feet. Mayhem reigned until the regimental picket arrived and marched some of the offenders off to the guardroom to face a charge next day.

Many soldiers never rose above this life of drinking, whoring and fighting, but to others, military service was a job which offered rewards. In such a context, a man like Willie developed a Jekyll and Hyde personality. He might writhe inwardly against the harsh discipline or the short rations. From time to time he would kick over the traces and embark on a wild orgy of drink and lust. But when the hangover had subsided and punishment drills had taken their toll, he would submit once more to discipline and training and find some point in them after all.

* * * * * *

In 1904, Willie was posted to India to join the ranks of British battalions who guarded the greatest of Britain's colonies. He set out from Dublin to join the 2nd Battalion of the Connaught Rangers. He was to remain there until 1910 and the experience was to work for good and ill in his future life.

We have no record of his trip, but Frank Richards, who had been posted to India some two years before, sailed from Southampton

---

[43] N F N Jourdain, *Ranging Memories*, (1934) p. 73. Reprinted by permission of Oxford University Press

on a troopship carrying nearly two thousand men. The voyage out by way of the Suez Canal took three weeks. Though sleeping conditions below decks were, for other ranks, almost as bad as the old slave ships, by day the voyage was something of a holiday from army routine. Drill was limited to one hour per day. The men whiled away the hours in gambling and, after the ship passed Gibraltar, slept at night on the open deck. On arrival at Bombay, the soldiers dispersed to their camps and stations. Willie was sent to Colaba and then to a station whose name is illegible in the army record. Thus began a process of upward social mobility which would eventually lead the young Glasgow labourer into white-collar employment.

The British army in India was just then undergoing a re-organisation that was aimed at converting it from an army of colonial occupation into a modern fighting force that could defend 'The Jewel in the Crown' from the threat of Russia. The Commander-in-Chief, Lord Kitchener, sought to concentrate his forces in the Punjab, towards the north of the sub-continent, and to equip them with modern weapons such as heavy artillery and machine guns. As part of this reorganisation, the army needed better-educated soldiers who could read and write competently and, among other things, transmit signals by telegraph and the new-fangled telephone. Since most of its home recruits came from the unskilled members of the working class, whose education finished at the age of thirteen and had often been interrupted by ill health and truancy, it was necessary for the army to provide an educational top-up before it could train them in the ways of modern warfare. Each military station had its regimental school for the children of serving soldiers. Since nearly sixty percent of recruits were either illiterate or barely literate, they were also required to attend at the school to attempt at least the third class certificate of education. Half of the men failed, even though the standard to be reached was only that required of a nine year old in civilian schools. In India, school was held in the afternoon when it was too hot to drill. According to Frank Richards, many men flatly refused to undergo further education, even after extra pay was introduced as an inducement in 1906. Willie was one of the few who persevered, passing the Third Class Certificate in 1904 and the Second Class in

1905. The latter took him to roughly the sixth standard, at which most civilian children left school, able to read competently from a primer, write to dictation and work out compound interest in arithmetic.

These qualifications brought him an addition of sixpence to his daily pay of one shilling. The award of two good-conduct badges accompanied them and promotion followed – first to lance corporal in 1906 and then to corporal in 1907. With the stripes came responsibility. He was undertaking supply duties at the great army station of Poona in the Punjab in 1907 and went on in the following year to train in field telegraphy and care of telephones in the field. This was a momentous move. It converted Willie from a mere foot slogger into the new kind of soldier, at the leading edge of science and technology, who would be so crucial to the winning of modern battles and wars. It secured him immediate advancement as a government telegraphist at Ambala, where he worked for two years, gaining a further certificate in the transmission of messages in Morse Code.

These early experiences in the army showed Willie Patterson the possibilities and advantages of self-improvement. It brought extra pay and little luxuries. The cost of living in India was far less than in Britain and a soldier could live well on his pay. The meat ration was larger and appetising extras could be bought from Indians who came to the camps selling milk, butter, bacon, eggs and fresh meat with Indian vegetables. Frank Richards found that everything was dirt-cheap and understood what the old soldier had meant when he called India 'a land of milk and honey'. Work was easier too, for there were Indian *wallahs* to clean boots and straps and carry out domestic duties. Willie, the rather wild young Jock from the back streets of Calton, began to see a brighter future in the army. He did not make the mistake of many young privates and fritter away all his leisure time drinking and gambling. Instead he grasped the opportunities for self-improvement which the army offered. Those who despised them did so at their own cost. A quarter of the British army at that time left it to join the ranks of the unemployed. Willie was not going to be one of them.

So the army fostered in Willie qualities which were thought of in his day as 'manly' – self-control, forethought and ambition. But the

Imperial Army had its darker side, which encouraged a man's brutal tendencies. Soldiers, especially NCOs, could become addicted to petty despotism and bullying. It was not for nothing that the early feminist, Mary Wollstonecraft, singled them out as the most grievous oppressors of women. India was a fertile breeding ground for such faults. Men like Willie, despised in boyhood as 'low Irish', soon learned to look with contempt upon 'natives' and developed despotic habits. British soldiers had little time for the 'niggers' who waited upon them in camp. The Viceroy, Lord Curzon, sensitive to the growth of Indian nationalism, frowned on such ways and Willie's generation had to be more careful in how they treated 'natives'. Officially, you could be charged for beating them, but older soldiers advised the young men to hit them in a soft place so as not to leave a mark. If the Indian dared to complain, no one would take his word against that of a white man.

According to the arch-Imperialist, Frank Richards, the Connaught Rangers had a supreme reputation for handling natives. They believed in the saying that 'what had been conquered by the sword must be kept by the sword.' Not being issued with swords, they used their boots and fists and were more feared by the natives than any other British regiment.

Along with despotic rule over 'native' men went sexual exploitation of 'native' women. The army ethos made this inevitable. Officially, the high command enjoined sexual restraint on the men, but it was widely believed among serving officers that soldiers could not be expected to live without regular sexual relief in the heat and dust of India. On the other hand, the military restriction of marriage meant that many men had to find consolation with Indian prostitutes. No soldier was allowed to marry before the age of twenty-six. Each regiment allowed a quota of up to seven percent of marriages 'on the strength', supported, that is, by additions to the soldier's pay and provision of married quarters. Other men had to wait, so to speak, for a vacancy if they wanted a wife 'on the strength', or else marry in Britain and leave their wives back home while they served in India for years on end. Liaisons with the wives of other men were severely frowned on. The soldiers' wives were said to be very respectable and any of them who took up with a 'fancy man' earned the severe disapproval of the Colonel's lady.

Not surprisingly, then, soldiers resorted to the prostitutes who hung around the camps and bazaars. Richards recalled that many men put money aside from their pay each week to spend on drink, tobacco and women. Women had long been available in brothels officially reserved for white troops. The army thought these reserved houses would regulate 'vice' and restrict venereal disease. Richards' account of the system shows how false these assumptions were. Especially notable is his description of the reserved brothel at Agra, where Willie's regiment was sometimes stationed. The responsibility for contraception and prevention of disease rested with the women who used familiar preparations. They were regularly inspected by the station doctor and treated if they were found to have venereal disease.

Thus VD was very rarely caught in the 'Rag', as the reserved brothels were called. Yet as a provision for safe sex, the system was ludicrously inadequate. The Rag at Agra had some thirty to forty women to service fifteen hundred troops. In practice, they catered chiefly for officers and many of the men bought casual sex with 'sand rats' – the horrible name given to prostitutes outside the reserved houses. These were usually organised and exploited by Indian pimps who lay in wait for soldiers at the approaches to every station and camp. Thus, many soldiers were driven to casual sex with Indian women whose poverty was even worse than theirs. Rudyard Kipling built many of his tales and ballads around the tragedies of such men in India. In his novel, Kim, the hero's father, an Irish soldier, took to opium and women and 'died as poor whites die in India'.

This great failure of the British army in the care of its men stemmed from the conventional attitudes of the time. Officially, the army denied the existence of regulated brothels after the mid-1890s. What men did in their spare time could not be a matter for army regulations. The best the army could do was to offer advice and opportunities for 'rational' amusement. Kitchener, the Commander-in-Chief in Willie's day, preached self restraint and healthy exercise – the standard public school prescription for the repression of sexual inclinations among young men. Boxing was compulsory and there were organised football matches for the men and polo matches for the officers. Men were exhorted to attend temperance and Bible classes.

These alternative outlets had some success in attracting men, but many were cynical about organised sport and religion. They spent their free time just lounging about, reading cheap novelettes or gambling. Sometimes they bought live hares, wild cats and even jackals from Indian trappers and set their dogs to hunt or fight with them.

As to safe sex, no one offered instruction in it, though rubber condoms had been on the market since the 1880s. Richards recalled that lectures on personal hygiene made no reference to them, though detailed instruction was given on the cleaning of teeth! No wonder, then, that about ten percent of the British army was in hospital at any given time with venereal disease.

Willie Patterson was one of them, but he was no poor white trash. His military record overall was judged to be good and his superiors certified on his discharge that he was sober and well conducted. After his first year in Ireland, there were no further charges of drunkenness on his conduct sheet. But my mother remembered him as a man who loved music and dancing. He must have found the climate and the discipline of India as trying as everybody else. His solution, when things got too hard, was to go 'AWOL' and charges of absenting himself without leave were a recurring theme of his army career. The records leave no doubt about the way he was passing his time on these occasions. In 1905, he suffered his first bout of venereal disease, spending forty days in the military hospital at Colaba with a 'severe' attack of gonorrhoea. He left hospital at the end of June, only to return for nearly the whole of July with milder symptoms of the same disease. These bouts may have undermined his resistance to fever for he was back in hospital a month later for nine days to be treated with quinine.

Ill health continued to dog Willie during the next two years. Fever returned in May 1906. In the following year, he suffered from orchitis, inflammation of the testicle, which appeared to have 'no obvious cause' but was probably related to the venereal disease. In 1908, he had three spells in hospital at Poona and Dagshai, the first in

February for investigation of a heart murmur which did not prove serious. At the end of the same month he was back, having his venereal sores treated, and a mere fortnight after his discharge, he was hospitalised at Dagshai where he spent no fewer than fifty-one days with the same complaint. Towards the end of the year, fever cost him another fifteen days in the sick bay, receiving quinine and tonics.

Willie's diseases were commonplace among soldiers serving in India and aroused no adverse response. The same is not true, however, of his other great failing, the tendency to go absent without leave. Leave was rarely granted to a soldier during the cooler weather, which lasted from October to March. The commonest exceptions to the rule were for approved activities, such as football competitions. Treated in this way, men were tempted to go 'AWOL', extending their holiday for a short time. Minor punishment was imposed for offences of this kind, but longer absences were regarded as more serious, verging on desertion, and could result in a district court martial and a prison sentence of up to six months.

Willie's military career suffered a serious setback in 1908 when he went 'AWOL' and was placed under arrest on 9 February, was court-martialled on 1 March, and thereafter reduced to the ranks. It is probable that the absence without leave was prolonged, since only serious offences resulted in courts martial. Perhaps Willie had taken off on a spree for the New Year, which in Scotland was traditionally celebrated for a month after Hogmanay. Escapades with women may well have been part of the frolic, for, as we have seen, Willie was again in hospital at the time of his sentence, receiving treatment for his venereal condition

After 1908, however, the venereal disease seems to have gone into remission for a time and he settled down to work as a 'government telegraphist' at Ambala. But in December 1910, he was back in military hospital with the diagnosis 'syphilis'. His service records show that he was then discharged from the regular army, returned to England and placed in the reserve. He was, in any case, only a few months short of the eight years he had undertaken to serve with the colours. Back in Britain, he received the standard treatment at Netley, a military hospital near Southampton, which had a specialism in venereology. Treatment took the form of mercury injections, a severe therapy which was thought to cure the patient at the risk of poisoning him. Cure was by no means certain, even when the patient survived, but modern treatment with sulfonamide had only recently been discovered and their use was not widespread until after the First World War.

Venereal disease was to cast a sorrowful shadow over the lives of Willie Patterson and his family. Yet in those days, it bore little disgrace among the ranks. In any single year, as has been mentioned, well over ten percent of the British army were in hospital with it. Many of the High Command accepted promiscuity as inevitable in a soldier's life. Such attitudes were deeply rooted in the military ethos. It was less than thirty years since the army had abandoned the attempt to impose compulsory treatment on prostitutes in British garrison towns under the notorious Contagious Diseases Acts. These Acts had been introduced in the 1860s in the vain hope of stamping out VD and protecting the army from its effects on fitness for duty. The 'CD Acts' had raised a storm of protest from feminists against the double standard represented by the compulsory inspection and examination of women but not men. The repeal of the CD Acts was followed by a moral crusade against 'the white slave traffic' in which feminists and others roundly blamed men for debauching women, driving them into prostitution and passing on venereal disease to their wives and children. In 1913, the feminist leader, Christabel Pankhurst, published in this vein an outspoken series of newspaper articles entitled *The Great Scourge*. The solution she urged was 'Votes for women, chastity for men.'

Some elements in the high command took up this exalted moral tone while ignoring its political content. Yet, little changed in military circles. In India, as we have seen, reserved brothels for European officers lingered on, albeit in a semi-official way. Things changed little before the First World War. It was then that the army, alarmed at the effect of VD on fitness for the front, began to educate soldiers in the dangers of VD and in the means of preventing their infection by the use of condoms. These had been available in their modern form since the 1880s but, so long as they had to be purchased from the station bazaar, their use by soldiers was uncommon. Frank Richards suggested that some soldiers in India went in terror of the 'sand rats', but others resorted to them frequently. It is important to understand the causes which lay behind this apparently irresponsible conduct – the discouragement of military marriages, the tedium of service life and the lack of preventive education. Sergeant Robert Blatchford came to realise that circumstance was more responsible for the conduct of men like Willie than sin:

> *It is not the men who are blameable: it is the life ... Barrack life is bad. Barrack life will be always bad. It is never good for a lot of men to live together apart from home influences and feminine influences.*[44]

Ignorance, poverty and lust conspired to drive young soldiers into unprotected and promiscuous sex. To such men, venereal disease was a fairly minor illness. There were so many ways to die in India – cholera, malaria, heat exhaustion and so forth – that VD was just another risk that many men complacently accepted. In the heat, dust and boredom, promiscuous sex was a form of recreation and venereal symptoms were probably not entirely unwelcome in that it provided an opportunity for rest in hospital. As to treatment, men probably believed implicitly that the mercury cured them (though its powers were judged by medical opinion to be uncertain.) At all events, Willie's doctor at Netley certified that he was fit for military service and Willie probably felt that he had sown his wild oats and gained a lucky escape.

It could not have seemed like that to my grandmother or my mother. The former, as a committed Christian, and the latter as a left-wing feminist, were to be, understandably, as horrified as Christabel Pankhurst by the kind of masculinity Willie exemplified. With two such different outlooks, domestic conflict was inevitable.

---

[44] Blatchford, *My Life in the Army*, p. 119

Chapter Five

War in Africa

' *... Britain ... fought not only for specific European goals ... but also for the security of her empire throughout the world.* '[45]

O nce back in civilian life, Willie lost little time in getting married. His choice fell upon my grandmother, Sarah Craig, always known as 'Sally', who lived up the same tenement close, 68 McIntosh Street, at the poorer end of the district of Dennistoun. They married on 17 November, in 1911, when Willie was twenty-seven and she was seven years his junior.

The birth certificate of Sally's first child, Joseph, shows that he was born five months after her marriage to Willie Patterson. My mother must have known this fact, but never referred to it, though she did represent Willie's courtship of Sally as a whirlwind affair, in which the importunate wooer swept the adoring young woman away by indulging her love of dancing and the bright city lights. According to my mother, Sally was a beauty, with raven hair and great dark eyes. Willie was no doubt familiar with the delights of the great city, in which popular amusements and cheap entertainment were already highly developed. Though commercial dance halls did not arrive until the end of World War I, there were many dancing clubs in the east end and in the Gorbals, where working-class people could enjoy their Saturday evening leisure. Alternatively, it was possible to have a night at the pictures for there were already no fewer than fifty-seven halls showing silent films. Afterwards, a young man with only a little money in his pocket could take his girl for fish and chips, or an ice, sitting in at one of the new parlours run by Italians. At tables, screened

---

[45] W R Lewis, *Great Britain and Germany's Lost Colonies* (Oxford, 1967) p. 157.
Reprinted by permission of Oxford University Press

by high partitions, the young couple could hold hands and cuddle discreetly – much to the horror of Calvinistic prudes on the City Council. Living at 68 McIntosh Street, Willie and Sally must have had opportunities for seeing one another in intimate circumstances, if only in the close or upstairs on the landing.

Much later, during my boyhood, my mother would sadly recall that Sally had been warned about Willie Patterson by a mutual acquaintance who pleaded with her not to throw herself away on him. What my mother did not know was that young women like Sally were at a considerable disadvantage *vis-à-vis* men in the Scottish marriage stakes of those days. Thanks to the heavy emigration of men from Scotland, there were ten females up to age twenty-nine for every nine males and it has been calculated that half the women in Scotland were unmarried at the age of twenty-five. Though the 'sex ratio' was more equitable for young women in the poorer working-class districts of Glasgow, men like Willie could afford to take their time, sampling the goods, while young women like Sally must have been anxious to win their approval.

Sally herself had no remarkable prospects. Her father earned his living by driving a horse and cab. He thus belonged to a group of workers comparable to the drivers of horse-drawn trams, from whom they had often been recruited. The modest wages of such men, about twenty-five shillings a week, barely allowed for a decent respectability. At twenty years of age, his daughter was employed as a power loom weaver in the woollen industry. Such female labour was low paid in comparison to men's. Women were not promoted, but employed as cheap labour and expected to leave on marriage. Sally was therefore ready for romantic attachment. She probably fell head over heels in love with the ex-soldier who had seen the mysteries of the Orient. There was no question in those days of living together out of wedlock and remaining respectable.

Willie at least did the honourable thing, marrying Sally before the minister in the United Presbyterian Church to which she belonged. After eight years of army life, he may well have wanted to settle down, building on the economic advancement made in India and raising a family. Whatever his inclinations, social pressures on ambitious young men to marry young women they 'got into trouble' were then very strong. We have no reason to credit Willie Patterson with anything more than outward conformity to the social code. The cynicism of Indian army life could hardly have failed to affect his attitude to women. He had been used to receiving domestic services from them in army stations and a young man, hoping to make his way in civilian life, must have been in need of a wife.

Nevertheless, he loved Sally after his own fashion. We need not condemn him too strongly if he told her nothing of his previous sexual history. It seems highly unlikely that any young man would have done so at that time and, as we have seen, Willie had reason to think that his syphilis had been cured. But 'murder will out' and, in the nature of these things, it would prove impossible to conceal. So Sally lived to regret her hasty heart.

To Sally, at the time of their marriage, Willie must have seemed a thriving young man. His marriage certificate records his occupation as insurance agent, which seems to indicate that he was trying to continue the upward rise from his labouring origins begun in the army. In reality, however, his prospects were anything but secure. Insurance agents occupied a precarious position between workmen and clerks. They were not paid a salary, like the latter, but worked their 'book' of clients for commission. Willie would have bought the 'book' from an outgoing agent for about twenty-five pounds, using his army deferred pay. Commission on the tiny policies which working-class clients could afford, could not have earned him much more than fifty pounds per annum. This was barely enough to place a single man on the lowest rung of the white-collar sector. Insurance clerks went to their work in black coats, struggling to reach, and keep up, a lower middle class life style. Insurance agents were not quite so 'pukha'. They turned out in one-guinea Macintoshes to chase business in a desperate race for promotion. Only a few would succeed, thanks to the rapid expansion of the industry, and the risk of failure was high. Still, Willie Patterson must have cut a figure in Sally Craig's eyes as he flitted in and out of the tenement closes, collecting the weekly contributions.

But Willie did not remain an insurance agent for long. According to his Post Office pension record he was appointed assistant-postman on 8 March 1912. This change of occupation was almost certainly a retreat and a disappointment, made inevitable by the birth of his son. A new insurance agent could reckon to make no more than an unskilled labourer's wage in his early years and promotion to a salaried post as inspector or superintendent might be a long time coming. The year 1911, moreover, was not a favourable time for earning commission. Clydeside was just emerging from a four-year-long industrial depression. It would have been far from easy to persuade those hard-working housewives to take out new insurance when their men had been 'idle' during that time. A living wage from insurance could only be a distant hope for Willie when a child was on the way.

On the other hand, a postman's maximum wage was twenty-five shillings a week. This was no higher than the general average for the time and took several years to reach by rising up a scale. But postmen were supposed to have advantages which industrial workers did not share. Half of the available jobs were reserved for ex-soldiers. They were said to be sheltered in government service from the unemployment which even skilled workmen suffered in Glasgow. At a time of expansion in the business, postmen had some prospect of promotion. As a military telegraphist, Willie, therefore, might have hoped to proceed to the 'indoor' work of sorting letters and sending telegrams. Indeed he had written to the GPO from Ambala in India asking to be considered for such a job. As the Post Office required, his application was forwarded by his commanding officer, but he was unsuccessful. It is unlikely that anything in his army record counted against him. The fact was that the British Post Office could get ample numbers of young women and 'boys' to work as telegraphists or sorters for low wages. No doubt Willie was disappointed to be turned down for 'indoor work' as a telegraphist and looked askance at the 'outdoor work' of a postman, but with a new wife and child, it was Hobson's choice. Quite simply the Post Office was the safer bet.

Promotion did not come quickly, however. Apart from the routine upgrading from assistant-postman to postman, which came in

January 1913, he was still working at the letter-carrying grade when his second child was born in July 1914. Despite public goodwill towards 'the postie', with his welcome knock and cheerful greeting, the postman's lot was not always a happy one. Backbreaking sacks of mail had to be carried up the long tenement stairways. At a time when letters were delivered more than four times a day, each delivery saw three peaks of rush and stress for postal workers. Duty rosters were arbitrarily arranged to meet these needs and there was a lot of compulsory overtime. At Christmas, men could find themselves working for twenty-four hours at a stretch and, at such times, postmen were often hassled and harassed by superior ranks. A system of good conduct stripes was matched by dismissal of postmen who stepped out of line.

It was much like being back in the army. As one contemporary commented, the Post Office was a 'snob inferno'. Counter-clerks and sorters in civilian clothes lorded it over the 'outdoor grades' who worked under inspectors exercising discipline like army NCOs.

The low pay of most uniformed men also meant living in poor quarters. We find Willie and Sally living, after four years of marriage, at 117 Garngad Road. This was the poorer end of Garngad in the mixed working-class district of St Rollox.

St Rollox had been the cradle of Scotland's industrial revolution and nursed some of the greatest factories and workshops in the world. The enormous smokestack known as 'St Rollox stalk' towered over the chemical factory of Sir Charles Tennant, whose daughter, Margot, was married to the British Prime Minister. Huge locomotives were built in vast railway workshops like Cowlairs and exported far and wide throughout the colonies. Around these belching smokestacks, clanging sheds and dreary slag heaps, great squares of tenement buildings, four stories high, housed the skilled artisans who toiled in 'the second city of the Empire'. Older and much less desirable tenements still housed some of the unskilled labourers and their families. One of these was to be seen in 'Tenants' dwellings' a notoriously overcrowded building at the corner of Garngad Road and Springburn Road.

When the Patterson's second child was born on 6 July 1914, they called her Sarah after her mother but she was always known as 'Sadie'. While Sally was giving birth, the world was plunging deep into crisis. The heir to the throne of Austria, Franz Ferdinand, had been assassinated in Sarajevo on 28 June. Austria issued an ultimatum to Serbia on 24 July and declared war, with German backing, on the 28th. Russia came to the aid of her brother Slavs and, by 2 August, all Europe was at war. Officially, Britain went to war to defend Belgian neutrality, which Germany had violated in an unsuccessful effort at a knock-out blow against France. Britain was committed, by secret talks, to help defend France against such invasion. Behind these understandings lay the British desire to protect her foreign and colonial trade. Had France fallen in 1914, Germany could have occupied her ports on the Channel and the Mediterranean, threatening the shipping trade so vital to industrial centres like Glasgow.

* * * * * *

When Britain went to war, Willie still regarded himself as a career soldier, only a few months short of his final discharge from the army. Hostilities having broken out, the Connaught Rangers could retain his services for a year beyond his formal engagement. On 4 August, along with thousands of other reservists, he received a telegram from the War Office requiring him to report to his regimental depot at Galway. His travel arrangements were pre-arranged and he had only to present his army identification papers at the railway station to obtain a warrant for travel to Liverpool. There he would have boarded ship for Dublin. A final rail journey across Ireland took him to the western seaport.

New recruits and reservists poured into the Galway depot and the commanding officer was busy raising a new battalion for service in France. On 19 August, Lt Colonel Jourdain, officer commanding the new 5th Service Battalion, Connaught Rangers, left Galway with his officers and NCOs for Dublin where the new recruits gradually joined him for training and embarkation.

Willie was not among these early drafts. While others marched off to foreign parts, he kicked his heels around the depot. There is no explanation for this in his army record, but it does strongly suggest that Willie was bored. As always when he had nothing much to do, he got into trouble and there were minor charges of misconduct. This time, however, they could not have been regarded as very serious, since he was promoted to corporal (thus regaining the rank he had lost in 1908) and on his discharge in October 1915, he was described as 'a sober and well conducted man' who had no recent charges of drunkenness against his name.

While in Ireland, Willie must have been giving thought to his long-term interests. The Post Office had done nothing to further his ambitions and the army was the only profession in which he had advanced hitherto. Back in civilian life, he might remain a humble postman on average unskilled wages for the rest of his working life, with no guarantee of a pension at the end. On the other hand, he could qualify for an army pension if he re-engaged with the Connaught Rangers and completed twenty-one years of service. Re-engagement involved obvious dangers, but there was no certainty of avoiding these in any event. By the end of 1915, the war was clearly settling into a lengthy affair. Hitherto, the government had relied on voluntary recruitment, but had failed to raise numbers sufficient for the Western Front. Many newspapers and politicians were clamouring for compulsory conscription which was finally introduced on 3 May 1916. Long before, Willie must have known that he would be recalled to active service, even if he took his discharge at the end of 1915. Such considerations may well have been in his mind when he applied to re-engage with the Connaught Rangers for a further nine years in order, as he told the authorities, 'to qualify for a pension'. The regiment refused to accept him but offered to sign him on for the duration of the war. Willie felt insulted. Why, after all, should he serve his country in danger and get no provision for his future as an old or possibly wounded soldier? He refused the regiment's invitation and took his discharge. But he remained disgruntled at his treatment. Never a man to knuckle down without a murmur, he wrote to the War Office, politely requesting an explanation. Army records show that a full report was demanded by them, to which the Infantry Record Office, Cork, replied simply that they had been bound to turn down Corporal Patterson's request 'by the orders governing this matter'.

Nothing more was proffered by way of explanation and Willie returned to Glasgow and his job in the Post Office. Any suspicion that his wish to extend his army service to twenty-one years had been due to estrangement from Sally must be dismissed, for she made him welcome. As a result, my mother was born on 12 November 1916. But there could be no lasting peace at the home fire for Willie. Universal conscription was coming ever closer. As in 1902, however, Willie was in no hurry to enlist. Two days after the final introduction of conscription, on 5 May 1916, he joined the Royal Engineers as a pioneer in the Signal Service. He was now back in the army to do the job for which it had trained him.

At thirty-two years of age, he was, as his medical record shows, still a well-set up man with a good physique and an inch or so taller than at first engagement. A posting to France was announced, but before it could take effect, his old complaint of orchitis returned to haunt him. He spent three weeks in hospital at Maryhill Barracks, which became engraved on my mother's memory as the place where he was 'sterilized'. Certainly, Sally had no more children and it is possible that sterility resulted from the disease. More to the point, it is difficult to see how Willie could have hidden his sexual history any longer from Sally. Its revelation would have come as a shock, raising the spectre of 'the great scourge' – a loathsome illness threatening her and any other children she might bear him in future. Indeed, the ghosts of the past may already have scared her, for little Margaret had had to have her eye sockets washed out, a standard procedure for various infections at birth, including syphilis.

Willie therefore had probably good reason to make himself scarce. Discharged from hospital, he was sent to an army camp in the south of England. A board of inquiry followed at which his posting to France was changed to another theatre of action. This was German East Africa, today called Tanzania, where British and South African forces had been struggling in the first two years. So my mother had not been entirely deceived by family tradition! Her father did have a military connection with Africa and even, as we shall see, with the Boers in a roundabout way.

* * * * * *

Britain's conflict with Germany in East Africa had deep roots. Back in the 1880s the region (which comprises the modern states of Uganda, Kenya and Tanzania) was nominally under the rule of the Sultan of Zanzibar, an Islamic ruler whose forebear had moved there from Muscat in the Persian Gulf. He held sway over some towns on the African coast, of which the chief was Dar-Es-Salaam, and a few settlements in the interior near Lakes Tanganyika and Victoria. His ancestors had grown rich on the trade in slaves, ivory and gold, brought to the coast by Arab and Portuguese merchants who exchanged them for guns and other commodities coveted by African chiefs.

Britain had long disapproved of the slave trade, but was reluctant to commit enough warships to suppress it in the Indian Ocean. Instead, she looked to free trade and 'legitimate' commerce to replace it. By the 1880s, British, French, American and German merchants had been trading in the region for a generation.

Germany now began to look with a jealous eye on British influence over Zanzibar and its East African hinterland. The German Chancellor, Bismarck, who had hitherto been opposed to German colonisation, summoned a conference of the European powers to Berlin in 1885 to discuss their future relations with tropical Africa. The conference promulgated an agreement, later known as 'the Berlin Act', which declared the lands of the Sultan to be a free trade zone and provided for the neutrality of Central African states in time of war.

While the conference was sitting, and in contradiction of these liberal ideals, Bismarck declared a German sphere of influence over the interior around Mount Kilimanjaro and a 'scramble' for colonies immediately developed. By a treaty of 1886, the sultan's sovereignty was severely restricted and the rest of the region was divided between British and German East Africa. The boundary ran from Lake Victoria eastward to the coast, leaving Germany with claims over a territory bigger then France.

The motives of the German Chancellor were complex. Colonial annexation was one way to secure support for his government, hard pressed by Liberal and Socialist opposition. A 'scramble for Africa', moreover, would foment rivalry between

France and Britain, distracting the French from dreams of revenge for their defeat in the Franco-Prussian war of 1870. Such calculations, however, presupposed direct rivalry between Britain and Germany over East Africa. German Imperialists looked to the region as a source of tropical foodstuffs, an outlet for German capital and an arena for German arms. Bismarck granted them a charter of rule as the German East African Company and, within a few years, the first German settlers were ensconced on tobacco and sugar plantations near the coast and in widely scattered trading stations in the remote interior.

The local Islamic population of ivory merchants and slave traders did not take kindly to Company rule. They resented Christian preaching against the slave trade, while Africans hated the forced labour to which they were put on the plantations. A 'holy war' broke out, which a German expedition, backed by British gunboats, put down with extreme severity in 1891.

Meanwhile, the Sultan of Zanzibar had granted the Germans a concession of all trade centred on Dar-Es-Salaam. In 1891, therefore, Germany assumed direct rule over the whole territory and encouraged emigration to the colony. New crops like coffee and sisal were introduced and railway construction from Dar-Es-Salaam to the interior was begun, with a harbour on the coast for ocean-going steamships.

German colonial rule was harsh towards the Africans. The concessionaires who ran the plantations on the slopes of Kilimanjaro or the Pare-Usambara mountains which ran eastward to the coast, were granted rights of trial over their African labourers. Severe flogging was common for malingering, while German courts imposed the death penalty for theft and rape as well as murder. Africans were forced to build the second railway line that ran from Tanga towards Kilimanjaro and native chiefs were expected to conscript men and women for work on these European projects. Failure to do so would result in the chief being flogged or, in the worst cases, a visit from the hated 'Askaris', African soldiers armed with rifles, whom the Germans recruited to enforce their will. Remoter tribes, often themselves warlike intimidators of their African neighbours, refused to wait upon the imposition of the Kaiser's law. In 1891, for example, the Wahehe rose against the Germans and annihilated a force of Askaris near their capital, Iringa. It took nearly a decade to subjugate the region with artillery and machine guns. Many other tribal wars had to be fought, of which the most dangerous for the Germans was the 'Maji-Maji rebellion' of 1905. It was crushed by 1907 by a scorched earth policy which left more than 100,000 Africans dead from war, famine and disease. These terrible deeds were long remembered and, as we shall see, influenced Africans to support the British against their German rulers when Willie fought there in the First World War.

* * * * * *

Though often irked by German economic competition in the Sultan's lands, the British government was far more concerned to keep European powers, especially France, out of Egypt which had been conquered and annexed in 1882. Through Egypt ran the Suez Canal, the high road to India. In the lands of East Africa were the sources of the river Nile, on whose annual floods Egypt's life depended. Accordingly Lord Salisbury, the Prime Minister of the day, encouraged the French to extend their colonies in distant West Africa, shutting them out of Egypt by threatening war at Fashoda in 1898. In East Africa, his grand plan was to prevent the spread of German power from Lake Victoria northwards, through Uganda towards the Nile. In 1887 the two powers agreed to respect each other's position in the region.

By this agreement, there were to be no further annexations in the interior, but British Imperialists like Cecil Rhodes had other ideas. They dreamed of creating a continuous strip of British territory from the Cape to Cairo. This alarmed Germany because it would block expansion of her East African colony to the west, where the riches of the Congo beckoned. Thus for a time, there was rivalry between Britain and Germany over the region around Lake Victoria. The focus was Uganda which the Germans coveted, partly as an obstacle to the ambitions of Rhodes. Salisbury thought the Cape to Cairo project far too ambitious and concentrated on holding the back door to Egypt as a manageable policy for the time being. In 1890, therefore, he negotiated a deal with Germany whereby the latter recognised Uganda as a British sphere of influence and Britain transferred to her rival the North Sea island of Heligoland, which had come to Britain with the Hanoverian dynasty in the eighteenth century. By this agreement the Sultan of Zanzibar was finally pushed out of East Africa and the island of Zanzibar reduced to a British protectorate.

The British now found themselves locked in competition with the Germans in the development of the region. German farmers were first to settle on the slopes of Kilimanjaro.

A German railway thrust out from Tanga on the coast towards Lake Victoria, where steamer transport would link up with Belgian railway development in the Congo. This state-supported development spurred the hesitant British government into subsidising the building of a railway from Mombassa to the shore of Lake Victoria, whence steamships would cross to Uganda. The 'Uganda railway' ran close to the frontier with 'German East' for many miles. It was constructed by thousands of Indian 'coolies', lured to Africa by the promise of regular service for a few pence per day. They sweated, suffered and even died for the British Empire, pushing the railway line through malarial jungle, across waterless desert, and over raging torrents. They were attacked by man-eating lions and African tribes who believed that the 'coolies' enticed their women into prostitution. But by the turn of the century, the British Empire was reaping the gains of Indian labour. Indian troops enabled Britain to crush a mutiny in Uganda. Indian railway workers attracted Indian traders who moved in to supply their needs. Along the line, Africans traded ivory, hides and fruit for cloth, beads and other goods from the coast.

Thus, as the twentieth century dawned, visitors to British East Africa were surprised to discover an outpost of British India. Indians ran the Uganda railways. Indian troops and police kept order and Indian clerks filled the lower ranks of the administration. But in the Kenyan Highlands, settlement by white farmers was getting under way. British and South Africans moved in to raise coffee, corn and cattle. They were allocated thousands of acres each, as free grants from the British government. This was, in effect, an occupation of the traditional lands of the Kikuyu and Masai peoples, which, like the

Maji-Maji campaign, left a legacy of bitterness that contributed to the Mau-Mau rebellion in the 1950s.

Protected, meantime, by a network of military forts, the farmers and planters of British East Africa quickly formed a colonial aristocracy, living in style on African labour which could be hired for twopence a day. The railway junction at Nairobi was gradually transformed into an imitation of an English county town, with elegant villas, brilliant flower gardens, cricket grounds and racecourse. Only the Indian bazaar and surrounding villages for African labour reminded them that 'England', with its troublesome democracy and labour movement, was far away. That was, in one sense, how they wanted it, yet they looked to the Imperial Government in London to bolster their privileges, demanding restriction of African land rights and an end to further 'Asiatic' immigration so as to encourage more white settlement. In their zeal to build up a 'white man's country' they pointed to the example of German East Africa, where Berlin seemed to spare little expense on its own 'new India'. After the 'pacification' of 1891-1907, the Germans had entered on a policy of 'scientific colonialism'. Hospitals and schools were built, catering for Africans as well as Europeans. Tropical medicine and veterinary science slowly tamed some of the ravages of tropical climate and disease. In Dar-Es-Salaam and other towns, the red-tiled roofs of the railway buildings contrasted with the corrugated iron of the Uganda railway and the army of African 'Askaris' was impressive at a time when 'British East' depended for its security on troops sent from India.

Thus British and German colonialists seemed to have settled down in peaceful rivalry on either side of the Pare-Usambara hills. The period of 'pacification' was over. Each side hoped for a long period of peaceful development in its own 'new India' which seemed free from the troubles of the old.

Suddenly, in August 1914, this illusion was shattered.

* * * * * *

When war broke out in Europe, the colonial authorities in East Africa were inclined to think that it had nothing to do with them. British settlers in the Usambara and Pare mountains mingled with their

German counterparts on the other side of the frontier in terms of friendly rivalry. But their unreadiness for war was not just a matter of pacific inclination. They believed that the importation of European conflict into East Africa would be disastrous for their situation. War between white men would be the opportunity for black men to rise up and avenge themselves on British and German alike for the 'pacification' of the 1890s. Destabilisation in East Africa would inevitably spill over the whole of the Great Lakes region, affecting alike the Belgian Congo and the British territories in Rhodesia and Nyasaland.

Consequently neither colony was well prepared for war. On the British side the King's African Rifles was a small force of African troops with European officers, consisting of less than four full battalions, scattered widely over the region. In German East Africa, there was a similar 'Schutztruppe' of mainly black Askaris with white officers, amounting to some 2,000 men.

When news of the German mobilisation was received at Dar-Es-Salaam, the Governor, Heinrich Von Schnee, pursued a policy of keeping his colony out of hostilities – as Berlin had encouraged him to do. But the Commander of the 'Schutztruppe', Colonel Paul Von Lettow Vorbeck, had very different ideas. A strong German nationalist and Imperialist, who had just taken up the East African command, he believed that it was a German soldier's duty to come to the aid of the Fatherland, no matter where he might be when war broke out. Even though the fate of Germany would have to be settled in Europe, he believed there was much he could do. By attacking the British territories in East-Central Africa, he could compel London to deploy troops from Britain and India that might otherwise be used in Europe or the Middle East.

Von Lettow had relevant experience of warfare. He had been present at the Boxer rebellion in China in 1899 and had helped to put down revolt in German South-West Africa in 1904-7. The latter had given him confidence in the fighting abilities of black Africans led by Europeans. Ambition and study had taught him to improvise and to coordinate men of different races and armed services. Thus, when the 'universal war' that he had long expected finally broke out, he threw himself into the work of mobilising and expanding the 'Protective Force' of the colony. When Von Schnee dragged his heels, Lettow took the executive power into his own hands and moved his headquarters from Dar-Es-Salaam to the northern border with British East Africa. From this position, the German forces occupied Taveta on the British side and began making raids on the Uganda railway.

The British colonial forces stood on the defensive. The Governor, following well-established tradition, appealed to London for Indian troops. In response, an expeditionary force was sent to reinforce the colony. Mere defence, however, could not be a permanent strategy. The German cruiser, Konigsberg, was operating off the East African coast and had already sunk a British warship. Ports in German East Africa could provide bases for more German ships hurrying to the Indian Ocean from the Pacific. It was vital to deny the Germans the use of their ports at Dar-es-Salaam and Tanga. Moreover, if the German colony could be captured, it might prove a useful make-weight in peace negotiations, its return giving Germany a motive to evacuate Belgium.

Accordingly, an expeditionary force was prepared in India and crossed the Ocean to attack the German colony directly. This invasion plan was ill-conceived and badly executed. When the mixed force of Indian and British troops arrived off Tanga in November 1914, they landed so slowly that they lost the advantage of surprise. Lettow rushed reinforcements down the Usambara railway to defend the town. The British force, almost completely ignorant of the local surroundings, got separated among the thick rubber and sisal plantations on the outskirts. The troops from southern India, who had never been to war before, bolted, terrified by the German machine guns. In the subsequent panic and confusion, the British Commander re-embarked his force after only two days' fighting and sailed up the coast to Mombassa in British East Africa.

The failure at Tanga posed a problem for the Imperial government in London. Safe communications between India and the Middle East were vital to the war against Germany's ally, the Turkish Empire. But Germany had saved her East African ports and the Konigsberg was still operating against British convoys making for the

Suez Canal. Nor was it good for British prestige that Africans should witness the humiliation of an Imperial invasion force by an army of black men led by German officers. Finally British and Indian forces were needed, every man of them, for operations in Europe and the Middle East.

In these circumstances the British War Cabinet hesitated and British East Africa stood on the defensive during the first half of 1915 while Von Lettow conducted more raids on the Uganda Railway. In July 1915, the British had the satisfaction of disabling the Konigsberg in her hiding-place on the Rufiji Delta. Their success was limited by the fact that the great ship's guns were removed for use as artillery by Von Lettow, who was also supplied with war materials by German merchant ships running the Royal Navy's blockade. These supplies, and the reorganisation of the German colony's economy on a war footing, enabled him to augment his fighting forces to a formidable extent.

But Britain was not the only African power with an interest in sweeping the Germans out of the continent. Back in 1910, the Boers had made an accommodation with their former British antagonists, which left them effective masters of the new Union of South Africa, at least so far as domestic policy was concerned. On foreign policy, they had their own sub-imperialist agenda which, being anti-German, suited Britain. Pretoria and London alike wanted Germany out of Africa. Accordingly, South African troops invaded German South-West Africa and occupied it by mid-1915. Pretoria then turned its attention to German East Africa. Arrangements were made for a large contingent of South African troops to form part of an 'East African Force', with European, Indian and African troops under a British Commander-in-Chief. Before the campaign could get under way in 1916, however, the British general fell desperately ill and had to resign. The Boer general, Jan Smuts, freed by victory in South-West Africa, now took command of a united Imperial force of over 70,000 men, drawn mainly from South Africa, India and Britain.

Smuts began by pushing Von Lettow out of British East Africa and then aimed to destroy his forces by dividing his own army into two columns for an enveloping movement. Like many other generals, however, Smuts found that strategy is easier to devise than to execute. Few of his troops were accustomed to fighting in the tropics. He himself lacked relevant military experience and under-estimated the difficulties. Disease took a heavy toll of men and draft animals. Tropical downpours turned forest tracks to mud and impeded the passage of his transports. Men, famished and weak with fever, marched and fought whenever they caught up with the enemy. But there were no decisive engagements. Von Lettow knew the country. His men were accustomed to the tropics and had better medical care. Neither Commander could risk the heavy casualties that a decisive battle would cost. As Smuts advanced, Lettow fought a series of rearguard actions, disappearing into the bush after each inconclusive stand.

By mid 1916, Smuts's forces had occupied Tanga. His second column pursued Lettow across the Masai Steppe to the central railway and Dar-Es-Salaam was occupied by September. Smuts might have halted to rest his troops. Instead he sent them south-east, in pursuit of the retreating German force, towards the river Rufiji and the port of Kilwa. Here the heavy rains of January 1917 brought fighting to a temporary halt.

Smuts believed he had practically finished the job when he relinquished his command to attend the Imperial Defence Conference in January 1917. From a South African point of view, this was true, for he occupied the northern portion of the German colony, which was richer than the south, and he had recruited a force of East Africans by expanding the King's African Rifles. These he intended, it seems, for police duties. But London had no intention of stopping here and drafted a force of black West African troops into the south-eastern theatre. During the lull of the rainy season, moreover, they raised even larger numbers for the King's African Rifles. From this point on, the East African campaign was, in large measure, a black man's war, fought under British and South African command, with British 'other ranks' in specialised units. Willie was one of these. Many were men whose health made them ineligible for service on the Western Front. Thus it was an accident traceable, ultimately, to his sexual past, which singled him out for a bit part in the great game of British imperialism.

Chapter Six

Finding Medo

*'Nor Mars his sword nor war's quick fire shall burn
The living record of your memory.'*[46]

This chapter forms an intermission in the history of Willie Patterson. It tells something of my safari in East Africa, which I undertook to find Medo, the battle field on which he won the Military Medal. Before setting out, I purchased a mini disc recorder on which I kept an audio-diary of the trip. That has enabled me to report the search for Medo as it actually happened. The other conversations are reconstructed with as much accuracy as memory affords.

* * * * * *

By this point in my writing, I had reconstructed the various contexts which influenced the formation of Willie Patterson's character: Calton; the Indian army; the British Post Office. Only one more remained: the First World War campaign in East Africa, particularly the action at Medo, where he won the Military Medal. Yet I now seemed to be staring at a blank wall. I did not know where Medo was exactly. It is marked on no modern map of Mozambique and mentioned in no gazetteer that lay readily to hand. Yet I could be sure that it once existed. Willie's service record gave the date of the action as 12 April 1918, and two independent sources located it at Medo: the reminiscences of the German Commander Von Lettow Vorbeck, and the British Brigadier-General, C P Fendall.

To admit that I could not locate Medo precisely would be embarrassing enough, but I also felt uncomfortable at not knowing what Willie had done for his decoration. The source for this

---

[46] William Shakespeare, Sonnets, No. 55

information would normally be the Medal Roll in the Public Record Office, but the PRO informed me that the Medal Roll for 1917 and adjacent years was missing. The only hope, therefore, was that I might find a reference to the action at Medo in the war diary of one of the Commanders, either of Willie's regiment, the Royal Engineers, or of his unit, the Imperial Signal Company. That would mean tracking them down in the PRO. Surely I would be able to find the war diary of the officer commanding the Imperial Signal Company at Lindi in German East Africa?

But how was this to be done? In its general printed guides, the Public Record Office warns all inquiring researchers that it:

> ... *does not undertake research for members of the public, but maintains lists of independent researchers who may be willing to undertake such research.*

Naturally, these 'independent researchers' would have to be paid. Fair enough, perhaps, but what about blind researchers? Should they have to pay for research which any sighted member of the public could do for free? Surely, I thought, they would stretch a point for me?

My first approaches seemed hopeful. I rang up and was transferred to a young woman who had been a student at Warwick University.

'I know your voice, do I not?' she asked. 'Are you the Dr Reid who gave such interesting lectures on historiography?'

'Great!' I thought, 'I'm in.'

I explained my problem and she undertook, as a personal favour to me, to search for the war diary I wanted and photocopy it for me to study at home in the Midlands. I waited, and waited and waited, but nothing happened. When eventually I rang her, she confessed that the search was more difficult than she had supposed and had decided to ask one of the Public Record Office specialists on the First World War.

Again I waited and again nothing happened. Finally I rang the specialist she had named and asked him point blank how he was getting on. He said he was very busy and it was a matter of finding time and he would try to fit it in as soon as possible. Again I waited. Nothing happened. So I decided to ring one more time. He was very difficult to contact on the phone and I had to try many times before I got through. It was by now crystal clear that he either could not or would not undertake my quest. This placed me in a quandary. I could make a great fight over it with the Public Record Office. After all, the Disability Discrimination Act had been passed in 1995. The Act made it illegal to refuse a service to a disabled person unless there were 'reasonable' grounds for doing so. It seemed possible that the PRO would be acting illegally if it refused to make reasonable adjustments to help blind researchers to pursue their aims. Yet I knew from experience how long this kind of campaign could go on and I wanted to get on with my book.

So I decided on a tactical compromise. 'I can understand you're too busy,' I said to the specialist. 'That leaves me with one alternative: to employ someone from the list of independent researchers you recommend.'

'Right.'

'Well, there's an issue there as to whether the PRO is acting within the Disability Discrimination Act, but as I want to get on, I'll postpone adjudication on that question.'

I was lucky in the person chosen from the list who turned out to be an experienced researcher on the war in East Africa. I agreed a contract with this man and he tracked down the war diary of the Royal Engineers and found that it recorded the award of the Military Medal to Willie, but nothing as to the conduct behind it. He then located the war diary of the Imperial Signal Company. Again the same disappointment: merely a mention of the bare fact of the award. As these sources provided interesting details about the operation of the Signal Company at Lindi, I went on writing the first draft of my next chapter.

During this process, it came to me that we might have been looking in the wrong place. Perhaps we should have gone to the high command: to the war diary of the Commander-in-Chief who succeeded Smuts, another South African called Jakob Van Deventer. I quickly e-mailed my independent researcher again and he tracked down the report which Van Deventer had given the British War Office at the end of hostilities. To my intense satisfaction, it gave a very full account of the battle at Medo. It also provided me with a detailed map of the Medo area, showing that the place lay south of the river Montepuez.

The road to Medo (author)

I now knew that Medo lay on latitude 13° S and longitude 39° E, just south of the river Montepuez on Van Deventer's map, but I still had no clear idea what Willie had done in the action. As one of the 'or' (other ranks), he was far too lowly to be mentioned in a report by the Commander-in-Chief to a Secretary of State. In fact, the whole thing was beginning to reek of the massive class divide which separated officers from men in the British army of those days. Officers had their deeds of bravery publicly recounted in the *London Gazette*. Some of those who won the Military Cross had it ceremoniously pinned on their tunics by the King. But the Military Medal, introduced in the war as a decoration for other ranks was, as we shall see, merely slipped into the post with a formal letter of cover.

* * * * * *

Long before this point was reached, I had conceived the idea of going out to Mozambique to study the field of action on the spot. I had read up as much as I could find about the kind of duties signallers were called upon to perform on the battlefield and hoped I could deduce from the lie of the land the kind of act which earned Willie's decoration. I therefore made up my mind to visit Mozambique and walk over the field where Willie fought.

But how was this to be done and how could I, a blind man, hope to visit the north-eastern margin of Mozambique? Modern guidebooks told me that the roads there are the roughest of tracks, where buses never venture and other vehicles do so at their peril. The region is still notorious for malaria and more travellers are killed by crocodiles than by any other wild animal in Africa.

'You'll never do it,' I was told. 'Nobody goes there: it's far too difficult.'

I have often found that, if I want to do something hard enough, the means of starting out will be found lying close at hand. So it was to prove in this case. I have a blind friend, Mark Pilbeam, who hails from Zimbabwe, a country which borders Mozambique on its eastern side. In fact, as I was to discover, Mark comes from just this borderland and had ventured into Mozambique on fishing expeditions with friends. One day in 1999, I was talking to him about the East African campaign and informed him of my ambition to visit the scenes of action. A blind man himself, he grasped the nature of my problem immediately.

'You want a reliable private guide, don't you?'

'Yes,' I replied, 'but I've no idea how to find one.'

Mark is a 'can do' person like myself. 'Leave it to me,' he said. 'I'm going out to Zimbabwe for a holiday and I'll ask around for you.'

People often say this kind of thing and mean well enough when they say it, but it is rarely wise to place a lot of faith in their good intentions. I knew Mark would have a go, but who would be so bold as to take a blind man he had never met into so inhospitable a region as I had in mind? I must confess that I dismissed Mark's promise to the back of my mind, assuming that the task would prove too difficult for him.

I was wrong. About six weeks later he rang me up.

'You know that trip you wanted to do to Mozambique – are you still interested?'

'You bet.'

'Well, I've found just the man for you. His name is Karl Wolf. He farms in Zimbabwe, near the border. He's of German extraction, born in Mozambique and knows your part of the country very well. He's always been very interested in the East African campaign from the German side.'

And that is how I came to plan an East African Safari with Karl Wolf, a white African, descended from pioneer colonial stock. He proved to be a meticulous leader of safari, a genius at improvisation and a fascinating travelling companion. He suggested we should use the month of August, after he had harvested his fruit crop, when coastal Mozambique would be cooler in the sub-equatorial winter. We would travel in his Toyota pick-up truck, not so glamorous as a 'four by four', but a serviceable workhorse for nearly all African road conditions. When we reached the sandy roads of the coast, where vehicles sink up to their axles, he would have his winch and shovel to get us out! He would bring along Antonio, one of his African farm workers and we would camp in the bush.

Fred, Karl and Antonio (author)

By the time I arrived at Karl's place in Old Mutare, Zimbabwe, the mystery of Medo had deepened. Karl had found it marked on an old aviation map of the region but, whereas Van Deventer's map showed it as lying south of the river Montepuez, this map placed it north of the river. A more modern map did not show it at all, but indicated a town named after the river and lying south of it. I knew that Fendall referred to a cluster of villages, including Medo, in that location and I was pretty sure that these had been swallowed up by a modern town, much as modern Glasgow had swallowed the village of Calton. Now we were about to go there and put my theory to the test.

Mozambique is a long, narrow country with a coastline of over 1000 kilometres on the Indian Ocean. The scramble for Africa in the nineteenth century left it with rather odd frontiers in the north. South of the river Zambezi, it is reasonably compact and well defined. In the north, the Portuguese debated its frontiers with the British territories that were to become Southern Rhodesia (Zimbabwe) and Northern Rhodesia (Zambia). The Portuguese wanted all the land lying north of the Zambezi. It was largely unoccupied by Europeans, except for the region around Blantyre, where David Livingstone had established his Scottish Presbyterian missionaries. They were in no mood to surrender the salvation of African souls to Catholics. When, therefore, the frontier of Mozambique was settled in 1891, the British (who called the shots) carved out the colony of Nyasaland (modern Malawi). Thrust like a spearhead down into the torso of northern Mozambique, Malawi separates it into two portions, one lying to the west of Malawi and the other to the east.

The old fort at Ligunia (author)

Setting out from Old Mutare today, therefore, it is not possible to reach north-east Mozambique, where 'Medo' is located, without first entering southern Mozambique, driving north to the Zambezi and crossing it at Tete, the site of the only bridge. We would then travel up to the Malawi border post. From there it would be a drive of some 200 kilometres over the Shire Highlands, through the Malawi capital of Blantyre, re-entering the Mozambican province of Zambesia. Even then, we would still be hundreds and hundreds of kilometres south of the town of Montepuez and the Indian Ocean ports of Pemba and Lindi, which I also wanted to visit.

* * * * * *

Karl packed his truck with camping gear and farm produce and we set out from Old Mutare early in the morning of 7 August 2000. We drove to Tete and crossed the Zambezi. We had hoped to reach

Malawi before the border post closed at 6 p.m. but a puncture on the road detained us and we set up camp in the bush about 60 kilometres north of the crossing point.

The author at first camp-site at Tete (author)

Next morning we drove to the border post and entered Malawi, speeding on over a good road through the Shire Highlands to the border with north-east Mozambique at Milanji. We camped for the night a little way inside Mozambique. On Wednesday 9 August, I woke to the sound of a woman pounding grain to feed her children who stood around her, wondering and laughing at the sight of these strange white people who had arrived in the night to pitch their tents in the gravel pit next to their hut. Their amazement was entirely understandable. We were in what Karl jokingly calls 'DDA', 'deepest, darkest Africa' where, even today, Europeans are a very unusual sight, and campers are as rare as birds blown in from another continent.

Our plan now was to drive south-east towards the town of Namucura, almost on the Indian Ocean mouth of the Zambezi. This was the farthest south point reached by the German army. From there we could explore in reverse the territory they and the British had fought over, visiting the hill town of Alto Moloque, through which the armies had marched, then heading for Pemba, a port on the north-east coast, which the British used as a supply base in Portuguese territory.

Mozambique suffered from a ferocious civil war in the 1980s and early 1990s. It was fought mostly in this north-east region and the signs of devastation were everywhere. At Namucura, we found the railway station where Portuguese and German forces had clashed in 1918. Everything had been trashed by the sabotage of Renamo guerrillas in the civil war. The dire poverty of the region was vividly illustrated by the huge crowd of Africans milling about aimlessly in the abandoned forecourt. There were teenage girls carrying babes in arms while young men horsed round about them. Young grandparents looked on and chatted impassively. Our arrival caused a great stir. They had never known white people to get out of their car as we did. I overheard one of the young women speculating that we might be from California. I did not have enough Portuguese to be certain, but quite possibly she thought we were a film crew.

From Namucura, the direct way to Pemba would be north up the coast, but the roads are very sandy and our heavy-laden truck would never have got through. So we retreated 150 kilometres to Mocuba, from which we could drive to Pemba on the 'better' roads of the interior. 'Better' is a relative term, of course. In this remote region, the roads are usually dirt tracks. Under summer rains, as Willie found, they turn into swampy rivers. In winter, when we passed over, they are pitted with potholes and strewn with boulders. We bumped, rattled and banged along these roads, often reduced to a speed of 20 kph. We found Alto Moloque in ruins but were rewarded near Alto Ligonia by the chance to photograph a Portuguese *boma* or fort, which might have been standing there since the First World War.

On August 11, we reached Pemba where Willie had disembarked with British troops to march inland on Medo. We intended to rest here for a couple of days with a friend of Karl's who farms coconuts on an offshore island in the Indian Ocean. But as he was not at home, we postponed our stay with him in favour of first visiting Medo and Lindi.

Accordingly, after a night's rest in a beach hotel, we again packed into the Toyota and headed inland as Willie had done in 1917. Our way lay along roads that were as rocky as dried-up gullies, through old plantations of kapok and cotton, some of them fallen into a wild state. We passed scenes of medieval aspect that might have come from a European fairy story. Here by the roadside was a charcoal burner, and there was a baker using a hollowed out termite nest as an oven.

As we approached the town of Montepuez, about 200 kilometres inland from Pemba, Karl saw a long ridge, rising about a thousand feet above the plain, and I realised at once that this must be Chirimba Hill over which, according to Van Deventer's account, the battle of Medo was fought.

On my audio-diary, I hear again Karl's commentary as we enter a suburb of African huts. We are greeted by a signboard proclaiming 'City of Montepuez'. Its civic pride is no empty boast. This is a town of some importance, by far the largest between here and the coast. In its vicinity, marble is quarried, cotton grown and timber logged. Among these rural industries are signs of modernity, even post-modernity. The main avenue, though but a dirt road, is lined down the middle by electric streetlights and a huge satellite dish dominates the skyline. To this market town, Africans come from surrounding villages to purchase their basic needs – foodstuffs, paraffin, sewing machines and spare bicycle parts.

We drive down the main avenue, lined with seedy bars and guesthouses, where you might pick up food poisoning or something worse. Karl is on the lookout for a filling station as he needs to get another puncture mended. We find it under the satellite dish. Out jumps Karl to see what's what and I wind down my window to listen to the sounds of Africa. As everywhere, a knot of children rapidly gathers round the truck. They stare wonderingly into the cab, exchanging muted inquiries with each other about its contents. From a bar behind the children, a television show raucously disturbs the peace. That, in part, explains the satellite dish. This is a regular metropolis by the standards of rural Mozambique. A heavy truck pulls out onto the avenue where motor scooters buzz about like angry hornets.

Karl returns. 'They all know Chirimba ... Chirimba Hill, it is right here, nearby. They call it Bennett ... They don't know the town of Medo nearby. My aviation map shows Medo north of the river Montepuez. Your military map shows Medo south ... I was told that this main road I have come in is in the vicinity of a thousand metres of Chirimba, i.e. back the way we have come. What I will have to do now is pick up somebody to show me where the hill line is and then I'll make plans where to camp.'

Karl goes off, leaving me sitting with Antonio on the filling station forecourt, in a glow of late afternoon sunshine. He picks up a young African to guide him in the truck to Chirimba. This young man, Michael, offers to guide us up the hill next day and invites us to camp in the yard of his boss who owns a sawmill. This 'yard' turns out to be grass covered, and is enclosed by buildings. Here we will be able to leave our camp set up tomorrow while we explore Chirimba Hill and look for Medo.

No one seems to know the true relation of Montepuez to Medo. When asked, they sweep around with an arm and say 'Montepuez, Medo.' They all know the name of Chirimba Hill even though they call it Bennett.

Michael comes from Tanzania. His father was a Pole and his mother Tanzanian. He has worked down here for a few years. He tells us that there is a 'pontoon' or ferry over the river Rovumo, which is the frontier between Tanzania and Mozambique. Karl is delighted with this news, for he has planned to leave Antonio with our camp-site on the Rovumo while we cross over and explore the region round Lindi.

In the yard, Michael introduces us to his foreman, tall, deep voiced, a man of presence, but very taken aback to be told that I am blind.

Michael hangs around for quite a time, offering us the use of a bathroom at his house. I wonder if he is hoping to share our meal. Karl goes on pumping him for information. In very halting English, he tells us that there is a road to Tanzania by way of Muedo and Palma. We will head that way after a couple of days exploring round Montepuez.

* * * * * *

Next morning is Sunday and a day off for Michael who brings a friend along for the Chirimba expedition. I am growing more and more certain that Montepuez has simply swallowed up Medo and other villages that existed in 1918. Karl is not so sure. We pore over his 1943 map, which gives Montepuez as situated at 13.8° south, 39° east. 'Mount Chirimpa' is shown just east of the town. We both think it desirable to establish the accuracy of Van Deventer's account, and decide to climb Chirimba Hill to survey the surrounding terrain. We think our guides are telling us, in minimal English, that the name Medo is interchangeable with Montepuez.

From the yard, Karl scans Chirimba Ridge through his binoculars and confirms that we skirted round it in the truck yesterday. Very bare and rocky, it dominates the whole area, Karl says, with a high peak at this end and dropping off to a low saddle, with a second ridge beyond. I am very glad of Karl's capacity for precise observation since, if I ever suspect him of coming to the wrong conclusions, he nevertheless gives me facts from which to draw my own.

After much debate and delay, we drive out to the eastern end of Chirimba Ridge and stand at the foot of the low knoll where the battle began. Karl is going to lead me onto it and explain the lie of the land. We leave the truck on the road and mount by a sandy footpath. There is no sign of the thick scrub of 1918. The path rises gently to the pass between the two ridges, with the knoll and Chirimba Ridge stretching away to the west. We advance up the knoll in single file, with one of the African guides close behind me and the other in front. I am panting hard, for I am rather out of condition after a fortnight of sitting on my bottom, and it is a steep scramble through tall thick bracken, requiring sharp turns and stiff pulls over rocky outcrops. As we approach the summit, the path grows easier.

Karl, himself an old soldier, comments: 'You have a very good defensive position here: huge boulders, and in the gaps between, you have sight of the sides of Chirimba Hill.'

North side of Chirimba Ridge (author)

He moves around, photographing the flanks of the ridge from various angles. I try to picture the general movement of the battle in my mind's eye from the vantage point, as it were, of the knoll. But for a time, this makes me utterly confused. I recall that the British troops got astride the Mloco road, running south from Medo. Karl seems to think that the Africans indicate the Mloco road running west to east. This makes us both rather puzzled. We concur that modern Montepuez has absorbed villages like Medo and Mueriti. But surely the Mloco road must still run south from Montepuez.

I suggest that we return to the truck and drive along the Mloco road so that I can get my bearings. Karl speculates that the Mloco road bends northward into Montepuez and that Montepuez is Medo. At this one of our guides says, with quiet emphasis: 'Medo Montepuez.'

'Quite so,' I think, for I am slightly irritated that Karl has taken so long to come to a conclusion so obvious to any historian of European towns.

Nevertheless, we concur that Van Deventer was right to place Medo south of the river Montepuez and that one of Karl's maps is wrong in placing Medo north of the river. This was the aviation map and Karl, himself a glider pilot, says, 'Aviation maps tend not to be too precise about towns because they are interested in river lines … and specific roads.'

'I think we've cracked it, Karl,' I answer, but my conclusion soon proves to be premature.

The author on Chirimba Hill with Mloco road visible in background (author)

From the summit of the knoll, Karl continues taking photographs. He can see a school and a mission station with a football field nearby. About two kilometres off, the Mloco road is visible as a thin line in the landscape. 'Do not confuse the mission approach road in the photograph with the Mloco road which is farther away,' he warns. This is the first I have heard of the approach road and I understand that he has just recently misidentified it as the Mloco road.

We descend from the summit, scrambling through a field of maize stubble, bumping on our backsides down the steeper rocks. Back in the truck, we head towards Montepuez. We are driving east-west, back along the approach road to the school, and the road is progressively turning further and further south. 'It shouldn't be doing that,' I think, 'if it is the Mloco road of Van Deventer's diary.'

The truck keeps close under the ridge until we reach its western limit where the road begins to turn south-west. I am even more confused now. If we are going south-west, how the hell did the British manage to go north to Medo?

Karl and I have a little brain storming session while the Africans sit silently impassive in the cab. He has forgotten his own warning about confusing the approach road with the Mloco road, as I have also.

Through my fog of confusion, I suddenly hear Karl say, 'I have to turn north to get to the river.'

'You have to turn north to get to the river? Ah, now I've got it. That's much, much clearer.'

But it isn't, for I immediately realise that we are now driving due south.

'Stop a minute, Karl. I want to talk to you.'

Another brain storming session, Karl sounding more and more uncertain of his bearings. Neither of us has any idea now where the Mloco road is, or which way the British went round Chirimba Hill. I recall the Grand Old Duke of York.

'Yet Van Deventer certainly says that they were able to get around Chirimba Hill on its southern side and get astride the Mloco road to the south of Medo.'

'That's where we've gone wrong. We think of them advancing along this road and we are calling it the Mloco road. But it didn't exist then. It's only an approach road for the school. For the British at that time, the Mloco road runs straight up from the south, north into Medo. There ought to be at least a modern equivalent today, running up to Montepuez.'

'Ye-essss,' says Karl, very deliberately, 'and here is the bridge of an old road right next to the hill!'

'Ah! There *is* an old road?'

'Ye-esss, running south from Montepuez, just where it ought to be.'

'Right, we need a photograph of that, Karl.'

If readers are now thoroughly confused by this game of blind man's buff, they will readily appreciate how difficult it was for me. It was only when I awoke at 5 a.m. next day, my mind sharp with early-morning clarity, that I fully understood how the land lay. What I had not appreciated was that we had approached the knoll on the south side of the ridge, driving along the school approach road. Remember, I did not then know of its existence and I had been naïvely imagining that Karl had taken me back to Chirimba by the road on which we had come from Pemba on the north side. As soon as I realised my initial mistake, the whole landscape fell into place in my mind's eye. We had to think of the British approaching from Pemba along the road we had come the previous day. They find Chirimba ridge, lying parallel to their road for two kilometres or so. They send a detachment up onto the knoll and another to go round the back or south side of the hill to get astride the Mloco road. They then face north and fight their way into Medo.

Thanks to Karl's prodigious patience, I had now found Medo. I could compare the topography of the historical sources with my newly acquired mental map, and to my great satisfaction, they tallied. I had still to puzzle out what Willie had done to get the Military Medal, but this question will be best answered after we have resumed the history of the East African campaign in the next chapter.

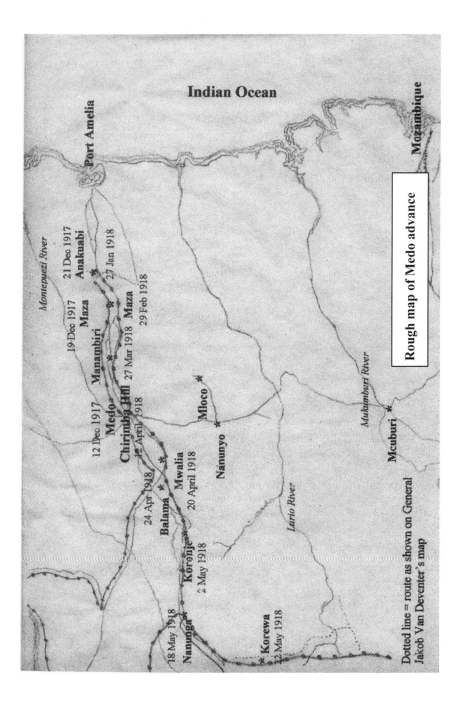

Indian Ocean

Mozambique

Port Amelia

Montepuezi River

21 Dec 1917
Anakuabi
27 Jan 1918

19 Dec 1917
Maza

Manaqubiri
27 Mar 1918 Maza
29 Feb 1918

12 Dec 1917
Medo
Chirimba Hill
12 April 1918

Mloco

Nanunyo

Mukamburi River

Mwalia
24 Apr 1918 20 April 1918
Balama

Mcuburi

Koronje
2 May 1918

Lurio River

18 May 1918
Nanunga

Korewa
22 May 1918

Rough map of Medo advance

Dotted line = route as shown on General
Jakob Van Deventer's map

Chapter Seven

The Battle of Medo

'Real solemn history ... with wars or pestilences in every page.'[47]

It seems unlikely that Willie Patterson would have paid much attention to the East African 'sideshow' taking place so far away in the tropics. For most people the war was in France and Flanders, where Britain and her allies confronted the German onslaught in a searing war of attrition. Yet, inexorably, an interlocking series of historical developments ensured that the man from Calton would be pushed into the colonial war, where Germany, Britain and South Africa battled it out for high stakes on the board of an imperialistic game. It is the story of that struggle and Willie's part in it to which we must now turn.

* * * * * *

At the end of chapter five we saw how General Smuts of South Africa had pursued Von Lettow's troops into the south-east region of the German colony, to the malaria infested swamps south of the river Rufiji. Once safely across the Rufiji, the German forces could not be pursued for several months. The rainy season swelled the current to a fast flowing flood, impassable, even for steamers. Roads were reduced to mud in which African porters sank up to their necks. The British forces occupying the small coastal ports of Kilwa and Lindi were in danger of being cut off.

General Hoskins, who succeeded Smuts as Commander-in-Chief, decided to call a halt and re-group. Kilwa and Lindi were supplied by sea during the rainy season and reinforcements were obtained from Britain.

---

[47] Jane Austen, *Northanger Abbey*, chapter 14

Colonial Building in centre of Lindi, 2000 (author)

Among these were Royal Engineers who provided men for the Imperial Signal Company in its new base at Lindi. One of their tasks was to train African and Indian troops in military communications, a complex field in which older methods of signalling with lights and flags survived alongside telegraph and wireless. Willie, as we have seen, was already serving in the RE as a pioneer and on Boxing Day 1916, he embarked on the troopship Nestor out of Devonport with a new East African Expeditionary Force. At Durban in South Africa, they trans-shipped, arriving at Dar-Es-Salaam on 26 February. Almost immediately, Willie succumbed to his old habit of going 'AWOL' and was deprived of six days' pay. We might suspect that the 'native quarter', with its prostitutes and brothels, lured him from the camp, but his medical record bears no entry on that account during two years' service in Africa. His other old Indian complaint, malaria, was a different matter, however. Soon after his arrival at Dar-Es-Salaam, he was hospitalised for more than two weeks with that scourge of the tropics.

* * * * * *

At the end of the rainy season, the British General, Hoskins, was replaced in supreme command by the South African, General Jakob Van Deventer. The War Office in London had been persuaded by Smuts that Hoskin's slow and methodical preparations were delaying the final mopping up of the German forces. Van Deventer had commanded Smuts' second column and the South African leader was eager to have a countryman in command so that Pretoria might gain influence over the carve-up of East Africa after the war. From mid-1917, therefore, Kilwa and Lindi became the bases of a two-pronged strategy. The force from Kilwa would drive the Germans south towards the Rovuma River, the farthermost extent of their colony, and the force from Lindi would be waiting for him there to bring him to a decisive encounter.

Old building on the beach near Lindi, 2000 (author)

By this time, Willie himself was at Lindi. The town had a small harbour, suitable only for sailing craft. As the men landed from lighters they saw a foreshore lined by large colonial residences and business premises. Behind it lay a small town of European-style houses fronting grass-roofed mud huts, home to some 4,000 Africans and a sprinkling of Arab and Indian traders. It was an unhealthy spot for Europeans, low-lying and close to the estuary of the river Luculedi, in whose swamps the malaria mosquito multiplied profusely. But it had been an important centre of German administration and settlement and was surrounded by well-cultivated plantations of rubber, sisal and palm oil.

Soldiers at Lindi, 1918 (Hugh Williams)

Because the harbour at Lindi was so small, steamships bringing supplies from Dar-Es-Salaam had to stand offshore and unload their cargoes into lighters. These were then towed up the Luculedi to Mingoyo, where the construction of a light railway had begun. There was fierce fighting round here from June to November 1917. Von Lettow's artillery shelled the troops as they landed, while British warships shelled the German positions. Spotter airplanes droned in the sky above seeking sight of enemy positions in the bush. There were terrific battles behind Mingoyo as the King's African Rifles, with their British and South African support troops, struggled to drive the Germans out of the Mohambika valley.[48]

Amid mosquito infested mangrove swamps, the pioneers of the Royal Engineers toiled to extend the railway and connecting roads. At the commencement of action in May, however, Corporal Patterson had been re-mustered from the 'Pioneer' to the 'Sapper' class and appointed as a 'field lineman'. This advancement, said to be 'for successful execution of a piece of work', entailed his transfer to 'special employment' with the general headquarters of the Imperial Signal Company at Lindi. It was not a comfortable desk job. Field

---

[48] There is a good account of this fighting by Brig-Gen Grady, 'Operations of the Lindi Column on 10 June and Subsequent Days', in 'Extracts from Naval Papers Lindi, June-Sep 1917', Cabinet Papers, PRO, 45/67

linemen were responsible for maintaining telegraphic and telephonic communication in the field of battle. They frequently went into dangerous situations, running cable from a trench or gun emplacement to an advanced observation post, whence information could be telephoned back. Willie would have worked on the maintenance of such communications at the front around Mingoyo. This is strongly indicated by his casualty record which shows that he was treated for malaria in the advanced hospital at Mingoya in August, and 'in the field' during September 1917.

A British officer who served in the same theatre left a vivid account of the toll which malaria took on a man's constitution. In the close and oppressive atmosphere, with the sun beating down mercilessly, he began to perform his duties listlessly. The hospitals filled up with exhausted, fever-stricken men, and he struggled on with just enough strength to 'stand to'. Not until he was actually unable to walk, was he himself taken to hospital.

By October Willie was back at base hospital in Lindi. This was lucky, for it meant that he missed the terrible battle of Mahiwa, where Von Lettow made his desperate last stand on German colonial soil.[49] It was the nearest thing to the fighting on the Western Front that either side saw in East Africa. Each side attacked the other's trenches with the bayonet, to the accompaniment of machine gunfire and artillery barrages. Casualties were heavy on both sides.

Strictly speaking, the battle ended neither in decisive victory nor decisive defeat. The British succeeded in pushing the Germans out of their colony, but Von Lettow refused to accept that his game was up. In November, his depleted army drew off to the south. Slipping through the encircling British troops, they crossed the River Rovuma into Portuguese East Africa. Lettow left his wounded to surrender and retained a force of 2,000 picked men and 3,000 African bearers.

His escape across the Rovuma was a serious British failure. They had set themselves to deny Lettow the crossing – and with good reason. The war was not going well for the Allies in Europe. Russia had collapsed in revolution. Germany could now transfer many troops

---

[49] Most of the fighting appears to have taken place at another village named Nyangao. C Miller, *The Battle for the Bundu* (London, 1974) pp. 283ff

from the Eastern to the Western Front. If she should break through, the war might have to end in a negotiated peace. Germany would no doubt demand the restoration of her East African colony. In addition, there was the future of Portuguese East Africa to consider. This ancient, ill-governed colony, until recently a centre of the slave trade, had long been coveted by Germany. It was rich in foodstuffs and military hardware. Lettow could maintain his army of picked men by seizing the forts and ammunition stores from the weak and incompetent garrisons. In the thick bush he might be confident of continuing to lead the British forces a merry dance until it was safe for him to cross back into former German territory.

Remains of German fortification at Lindi, 2000 (author)

London therefore decided that he must be pursued. They pulled out their Indian, British and Nigerian troops and sent after him a greatly expanded force of the King's African Rifles. Besides its

European officers and NCOs, it was accompanied by specialist British troops, including signallers. Willie, therefore, went with them.

* * * * * *

Van Deventer, Like Hoskins before, decided to use the rainy season to re-group and concentrate his forces in Portuguese East Africa. A base was established at Port Amelia (modern Pemba). Thousands of men and supplies were shipped down the coast from Lindi under the command of General Edwards. With them went Willie Patterson, whose service record shows that he was attached on 1 April 1918 to the signal reserve.

Edwards' 'pamforce' was intended to operate in conjunction with Portuguese troops and a second British column under General Northey which was approaching from the west. The aim was, once again, to encircle the German force and bring it to final conclusions.

As usual, Von Lettow had other ideas. Shortly after crossing the Rovumo, his men had captured their first Portuguese fort. Buoyed up by new supplies of food and ammunition, they drew off to the south. Lettow turned the main column west, to face Northey, leaving a detachment at Medo, a village just south of a crossing point on the River Montepuez. The detachment was to cover him against Edwards' column advancing from Pemba to Medo, hoping to drive the Germans into the arms of Northey's force. The result was another fierce clash in which Willie played a distinguished part.

The Germans had placed two companies on Chirimba Hill, a rocky ridge some thousand feet high and about a mile long,[50] overlooking the road from Pemba by which the British force had to approach Medo. On 10 April, in a night battle, an advanced guard under Colonel Rose seized a knoll at the eastern end of the ridge. Next day, a column under Colonel Giffard was sent round Chirimba Hill with orders to get astride the Mloco road running south from Medo.

Standing that day on Chirimba Hill (as described in the last chapter) and reading Van Deventer's flat prose, I had to make an effort of imagination to realise the horrors of battle and Willie's part in it. The thick bush which then clothed its slopes has gone, burned off

---

[50] Van Deventer to Secretary of State for War, PRO, WO 158/444, 1919, p. 8

by a much enlarged population desperate for fuel. Yet the pull up the rocky knoll at the eastern end is still a stiff one and would have been harder for men carrying forty-pound packs, rifles and ammunition. In the darkness of the bush at night, they must have stumbled and groped their way, strafed by fire from the summit of the knoll. Next day, they pushed on, gaining the ridgeback and fighting along it towards Medo in the west, where they joined up with Giffard's force. Van Deventer wrote a narrative of the day's events:

> *This movement was carried out successfully, but had been anticipated by the enemy, who kept half his force well to the west of Chirimba Hill in readiness to meet the turning movement.*

Colonel Giffard, on reaching the Mloco road on the morning of the 12th, turned north to attack Medo, but was counter-attacked in thick bush by three enemy companies which were later joined by another. From 1.30 onwards, fighting was heavy and close, but all enemy attacks were repulsed. Meanwhile, Colonel Rose, driving back the two companies holding Chirimba Hill, occupied Medo. At 5.20 p.m., he joined hands with Giffard, but the enemy got away before further attacks could develop. Casualties had been fairly heavy on both sides.[51]

Willie's service record shows that he was involved in the heavy and close fighting of 12 April for which he was awarded the Military Medal, 'in recognition of conspicuous gallantry in action and devotion to duty'.[52] Thanks, however, to the class system (as previously stated) that dominated the British army, we are told nothing in detail of Willie's part in the battle. The London Gazette duly reported his decoration, following its normal practice of omitting detail concerning the courage of the 'other ranks'. Officers got full citation of their deeds. The working-class lads, who were taken from the smoke begrimed cities to fight for the Empire in distant lands, were honoured only with the faintest praise. For Willie Patterson there would be no investiture by Royalty at Buckingham Palace. Such

---

[51] Van Deventer to Secretary for War, p. 9
[52] War Diary, Imperial Signal Company, PRO, WO 95/5315, 27 May, 1918

distinction was reserved for those who won the Military Cross, itself a decoration confined to officers. The Military Medal, which had been introduced belatedly as a decoration for 'the men', was sent to Glasgow by registered post, accompanied by a coldly official note:

> *Sir,*
> *I am directed to transmit the accompanying Military Medal which has been awarded to you in respect of your services with the Royal Engineers.*
> *I am to request that you will be so good as to acknowledge the receipt of the decoration on the attached form, which is to be returned to the above address in the enclosed addressed envelope, which needs no stamp.*

My visit to the scene, knowing the role that signallers played in such actions, suggested something of Willie's part in the battle of Medo. Rose's assault on the German positions on Chirimba Hill was a classic situation for cooperation between artillery and signallers. British gunners down on the plain would have been unable to see their targets on the bush-covered ridge. Signallers therefore moved forward in the teeth of the German machine gunfire to send back the vital information for range finding. Willie's Indian training in field telephony came into its own and his stubbornness in sticking to his forward observation post might have been what earned him the decoration for 'devotion to duty'.

For the British, however, it was to be another hollow victory. Lettow had had no intention of holding Medo. His strategy was to draw his enemies farther and farther south into the Portuguese colony. Leaving the Medo detachment, he moved west against Northey's column making its way east. He could hear heavy sounds of firing as he marched off.

From Van Deventer's narrative and the published memoirs of other officers, we gain an impression of the pursuit and its hardships. Edwards column found that progress was very slow:

> *The country was exceedingly difficult, the jungle being so thick that roads were mere tunnels through bamboo thickets and elephant*

grass, while long stretches of track appeared more suitable for boats than for motor transport.[53]

The thick 'black cotton' soil of the region turned into mud and swamp in the rainy season. Progress through it was slow and sapped the men's energies, or as much as was left to them by tropical diseases. Willie himself had only recently recovered from malaria when the Medo action took place. Communications were extremely difficult, partly because the British had decided to leave their wireless equipment back at Lindi. In many places, thick bush hid the enemy and even comrades from one another. The danger that they would stumble upon one of the German patrols, hiding like a leopard in the scrub, spitting fire from their Maxim guns, was very great.

Von Lettow had, to all intents and purposes, turned into a guerrilla commander, elusive and dangerous. His Askaris were experienced bush fighters, superior to the recent recruits of the King's African Rifles. Time and again, they took the Imperial troops by surprise, or slipped away unseen when they tried to encircle them with larger numbers. On top of all this, the Portuguese were a feeble force. Their soldiers, African and European, were sick and hungry and deserted in droves. Their transport arrangements were also chaotic.[54]

In May, General Edwards' force, in hot pursuit of the Germans, took them by surprise at the Koroma Mountain, and nearly captured the former Governor of German East Africa. Only Lettow's vigorous action saved the day and he again gave the British the slip. He marched south into fertile country along the river Malema where there were abundant tomatoes, bananas, sweet potatoes and other fruits. There was also plentiful game, so that his exhausted men recuperated quickly. Captured dispatches of General Edwards allowed him to slip out of the ring of advancing British troops as they closed in. Yet the thick bush was as much of a hindrance to the German Commander as to his enemies. However carefully he watched for gleams of campfires by night or clouds of dust by day, there were too few observations to follow a column properly in the right direction.

---

[53] Van Deventer to Secretary of State, p. 9
[54] PRO, Cabinet Papers, 4571

Thus the opposing armies beat about the bush and blundered into one another from time to time. The local African population welcomed the German force as deliverers from their Portuguese exploiters. Lettow therefore pressed on through June and July, threatening the port of Quelimane. He put British forces to rout on the Namacurra River, where many were drowned, including their commanding officer.

Well supplied with captured ammunition and stores, Lettow now made a break for German territory. Marching north, raiding Portuguese forts for supplies as he went, he inflicted a disastrous defeat on the KAR sent to block him at Namirru, where the English colonel in command was captured. On taking a British telegraph station, he discovered the existence of a large store at Fort Namura which he immediately attacked and took after very fierce fighting. Avoiding the swamps around Lake Nyasa, he pushed on over mountainous terrain, scrambling over ravines and slithering down precipices. Many of his best officers had been killed or wounded and influenza was taking its toll of his followers. African guides led him through thick bush to the Rovuma, Deventer's troops blundering after. On 21 September 1918, he re-crossed the river and slipped past the British at Lindi. Turning west, he skirted round the southern end of Lake Tanganyika, entering Northern Rhodesia. Black allegiance to the British was breaking down here and Lettow would have had little difficulty in holding out against a small force of KAR, but news arrived of the armistice in Europe on 11 November, and Lettow surrendered in accordance with orders.

The British military administration in German East Africa treated him with full military honours. He was taken to Dar-Es-Salaam, where everyone was anxious to see him. One British officer present at the scene described him later as 'a tall, spare, square-shouldered man, with close-cropped grey hair, and a clear eye which looked you straight in the face.'[55] He was largely exonerated from suspicion of complicity in the brutality which German troops and administrators had shown towards prisoners and non-combatants.

---

[55] Fendall, p. 128

His Askaris and German NCOs did not fare so well. Many of them died as they were being shipped by boat and rail to their homes during the world epidemic of influenza in 1918.

In the British East African Force, there was some criticism of Van Deventer for failing to round up Von Lettow's men in Portuguese territory. All things, considered, however, the allies concluded that it was the country that had beaten them. Quite apart from its adverse geography, Portuguese officials on the spot had proved extremely reluctant to allow Africans to work as porters for the British force, fearing that superior British pay would further increase their discontent with the rapacious rule of their Iberian masters. It is said that they murdered African village headmen who collaborated in this way with their own allies. What they did to those who welcomed the Germans as liberators is not recorded.

And what of Willie? It is impossible to follow his precise part in this war of blunders. He was far too lowly a 'ranker' to merit a mention in the Commander's war narrative. Published memoirs are often vague about the dating of events in which their authors played some part. Finally Willie's army record, though specific about medical treatments, promotions and awards, and the dates on which they took place, is sometimes silent about place names. When they are given, they are usually very difficult to identify and do not always match up with the names of battles in the other sources.

Yet it is clear that he must have been a courageous and valuable soldier. Signallers were at a premium when so much reliance was placed on the telegraph and so much wire was destroyed by the enemy. Given the circumstances of the campaign, he could have had few opportunities for indulging his weakness for women. His tendency to run a little wild when bored must have been curbed in the bush, far from towns and cities with their distracting amusements. In any case, regular soldiers were often the kind of men who stick staunchly to duty under conditions of danger and hardship, yet kick over the traces when they have to face only 'bull' and boredom. Ironically, among all the sources which say so little about the rank and file, it was one of Willie's German enemies who caught this side of military psychology, while comparing black and white soldiers.

Soldiers of either race were, he concluded, much the same. There were men with whom it was a pleasure to work and misfits who always get into trouble or get drunk. But he added that it was often the awkward squad who made the best fighting soldiers.[56]

Corporal Albert Williams, who served in Willie's regiment (Hugh Williams)

Far from garrison duty at home, Willie was in the field as a lineman with the signallers in Portuguese East Africa until Lettow quit the territory in September 1918. Shortly after the action at Medo, he was promoted to sergeant 'without pay'. He must have covered much the same territory as Von Lettow who, ironically, was able to attack Fort Namurroe by following fresh copper telegraph wire that British linemen had erected to ease communications on their own side. In June, Willie was laid up in an advanced hospital again with malaria. By early November, he was back at Mingoya near Lindi, but was unfit to continue in the pursuit of Lettow for he was again down with the disease. As soon as the war ended in Europe, he 'reverted', in the words of his army record, 'to corporal on ceasing to be specially employed'. At the end of November, the Imperial Signal Company was officially disbanded and Willie left Lindi for Dar-Es-Salaam. It was again a haven of peace – if not quite in the sense which the old Arab traders had meant when they gave it that name. Invalid British soldiers strolled about in blue uniforms, welcome replacements for the rags to which service had reduced them in the bush. Many adored Dar-Es-Salaam, with its white sand and wide avenues shaded by palm and mango trees. Willie was allowed a brief respite in this colonial haven

---

[56] H Fonck, *Deutsch Ost-Afrika: Eine Schilderung deutscher Trapen nach zehn Wandeq'ahren* (Berlin, 1907), p.69, quoted by L H Gann and P Duigan, The Rulers of

from 18 November until 21 December when he embarked per HT Ingoma for England. Demobilisation followed on 22 May 1919. His East African adventure was at an end.

* * * * * *

In retrospect, the East African campaign came to look like a 'sideshow' of the First World War. As memory focused on the vast slaughter of the Western Front, the Indians, Africans and British who had borne the pains of that 'poisonous country' were all but forgotten. Even today, it is only possible to give approximations of the total fatalities. The British forces lost over ten thousand men, two thirds of them from disease. German losses were about 2,000. But the black people of East Africa suffered far more as carriers who died from disease, exhaustion and military action. No one bothered to record their fate. One modern estimate is 100,000 dead on all sides. Black civilians also suffered dreadfully. War devastated many localities, bringing hunger, disease and death in its train. Thousands of Africans perished in the outbreak of influenza that swept over their continent at the end of the war. To some Africans at least, long stigmatised as 'savages' by Europeans, it was plain that there was often a savage behind the white man's mask of civilisation.

Memory of the campaign soon faded. One or two survivors, like Francis Brett Young, wrote up their adventures and Von Lettow was regarded for a time as a hero on the German side, like Lawrence of Arabia on the British. In our own time, the war in which they suffered has been rediscovered as black comedy in William Boyd's novel, *An Ice Cream War*.

A full history of the campaign, based on German, Belgian and South African sources as well as British, has had to wait until very recent times.[57] It shows that, far from being just a 'sideshow', there was a good deal at stake for contemporary rulers of the British Empire and their South African collaborators. They saw German East Africa as a potential base for the resurgence of German power. Unless it was denied to them, its ports and soil could be turned into submarine bases

German Africa, 1884-1914 (Stanford, Ca, 1977) p.159
[57] H Strachan, *The First World War, I: To Arms* (Oxford, 2001) ch 7, Pp. 569-643

and airfields from which to attack India and the southern dominions. In British hands, however, German East Africa would restore the 'missing link' that would complete the Cape to Cairo railway and would provide a landing stage for aircraft flying from London to Pretoria. These considerations grew ever stronger in 1917-18 as the possibility of the war ending in stalemate and a negotiated peace seemed to increase. Even in victory, they shaped the African colonial settlement hammered out at the peace conference in 1919. No British statesman doubted that the war was a struggle of Empires and many believed that, if Germany were denied her goal of dominating 'Mitteleurope', she would seek compensation in 'Mittelafrika'. With hindsight, such grandiose schemes seem fantastical, products of the over-heated imagination of Imperialists like John Buchan. Yet, as William Roger Louis has shown,[58] they were taken seriously at the time and this explains the tenacity with which British and South African forces pursued Paul Von Lettow Vorbeck and his Schutztruppen for four years across a terrain as large as Western Europe. It also explains why Willie Patterson's war was not the static confrontation of the Western Front, but more like a throwback to North America in the eighteenth century, where indigenous Americans fought each other in support of rival French and British claims to their land. There was no shortage of writers to turn the campaign into romance, just as Fenimore Cooper had done for North America in novels like *The Last of the Mohicans*. But the romance of East Africa faded, as we have seen, and Willie returned with a legacy of malaria to a home where warfare was soon to be regarded by many as a curse.

---

[58] William Roger Louis, *Great Britain and Germany's Lost Colonies, 1914-1919* pp.2f (1967). Reprinted by permission of Oxford University Press

Chapter Eight

'Red Clydeside'

'I rise up at the singing of a bird
And scarcely knowing slink along the lane,
I dare not give a soul a look or word
Where all have homes and none's at home in vain.'[59]

The return from war, as Edmund Blunden knew, is often very stressful for soldiers and their families. Military life tends to promote intense male bonding. Shared hardships and dangers, mutual support through long periods of boredom and depression, and moments of intimate comradeship between 'pals', induce a sense of unity, so close as to be seen by some commentators on the First World War as 'homo-erotic.'[60]

We know nothing of the way war worked like this for Willie Patterson, but the kind of experience he must have known is vividly conveyed in the personal diary of Eric Thompson.[61] He was a young South African machine gunner who served under Van Deventer in German East Africa from 1915 to 1917. His diary has recently been published in the *Journal of South African Military History* and vividly illuminates the life of war in camp, in field hospitals, on the march and under fire. The crucial importance of his close pals (his 'primary group', as sociologists of war have it)[62] is unmistakable. Thompson and his pals cooked for one another in camp, washed each other's

---

[59] Edmund Blunden, '1916 Seen from 1921' in E Blunden, *The Poems* (1930)

[60] P Fussell, *The Great War and Modern Memory* (Oxford, 1992) pp. 270ff

[61] Col E S Thompson, 'A Machine Gunner's Odyssey Through German East Africa: The Diary of E S. Thompson' *South African Military History Society Journal, Vol 7, No. 3-6,* 1987

[62] J Bourne, 'The British Working Man in Arms', in H Cecil and B H Liddle (eds), *Facing Armageddon: The First World War Experienced* (London, 1996) pp. 345f

clothes and cleaned each other's kit. A much-appreciated intimacy was shaving one another.

He greatly valued the letters and visits he received from his comrades when he spent six weeks in a field hospital, recovering from an accidental burn. These, and the comradeship he formed with other patients, helped to get him through a painful episode away from his machine gun section. One evening, the patients cooked and shared two chickens which one of them had bought. They enjoyed a good dinner and sat long in the tent afterwards, smoking and talking about things they loved, especially music.

Back in camp, there were high jinks reminiscent of schoolboy days. A patient from another tent came in one evening and started a 'rough and tumble' which disordered the beds and ground sheet. Later, the patients in Thompson's tent returned the compliment. The diary records that he slept well after that.

Soldiers spoke little to others about these aspects of army life, and British convention did not encourage much by way of revelation. It took a major French novelist, Gustave Flaubert, to discern, long before 1914, the intimate side of war:

> *The community of their lives had brought about profound friendships among these men. The camp, with most, took the place of their country; living without a family, they transferred the needful tenderness to a companion, and they would fall asleep in the starlight side by side under the same cloak. And then in their perpetual wanderings through all sorts of countries, murders and adventures, they had contracted strange loves – obscene unions as serious as marriage, in which the stronger protected the younger in the midst of battles, helped him to cross precipices, sponged the sweat of fevers from his brow, and stole food for him, and the other, a child who had been picked up on the roadside, and had then become a mercenary, repaid this devotion by a thousand delicate attentions and wifely kindnesses.[63]*

* * * * * *

---

[63] Gustave Flaubert, *Salambo* (Braille edn, London, 1941) vol. 4, 91-92

Such experiences could not have been entirely foreign to Willie, and the pain of separation from old comrades, either by death on the campaign or by demobilisation, must have been as real, if not as acute, as that described by Blunden and others. In these circumstances, return to a loving wife and routine employment would have been very problematic. Much would have depended on the former strength of the marriage and the changes wrought in the wife by war. As we have seen, the chance of Willie receiving a warm embrace from Sally was not very great. The pain of discovering the facts and consequences of his sexual history had probably not diminished since 1916. The experience of living for two years without him would have further weakened the bonds of their marriage. By all accounts, Sally was a strong woman. Life as a factory worker before her marriage must have acquainted her with the rougher side of things. That the war also helped to turn her into a wife who was quite capable of using plain common sense, strength of character and basic education to cope with trials, without the support of a husband, is suggested by the one piece of writing that has survived from her hand. It is a letter, probably written in 1916 and addressed to the regimental authorities, which was found among Willie's service papers.

> *To the Paymaster, Royal Engineers,*
> *Dear Sir,*
>
> *Would you be as kind as forward my baby's birth lines as I require them for next week you received them at the end of Nov in respect of my Maternity Claim which has never came forward as yet*
>
> *I am, Sir,*
> *yours etc*
> *Mrs S.C. Patterson*
> *Husband 161472 Lce corpl Patterson Presently stationed at Stephenage*

It is unlikely that Sally believed that Willie had behaved like a plaster saint during his sojourn in Africa, yet, for the sake of her children, she might have been prepared to patch things up. Certainly, my mother remembered her early years at Millerston as an idyllic time, when she was taken for rides round the park in a horse and trap by a lady who lived at Provan Mill. This memory may, of course, have related to a time before Willie's return from the war, but there was also a memory of him buying a piano for the 'back room', where he and his pals would practise the dance tunes of the day. My mother, who loved ballroom dancing all her life, always acknowledged her father's dancing skills. Once, as a young man, I got her up to dance. 'You're a good dancer, Freddie,' she remarked. 'You get that from your grandfather.'

According to my mother, she was her father's favourite child. Tomboyish in her ways, she preferred climbing and scrambling onto the washhouse roof with her brother Joe to any of the conventional girlish games. But it is also clear from my mother's memories that there were tensions. Willie, like many army sergeants, was a wilful, domineering man, accustomed to giving orders and being obeyed. For two years, he had been waited on by African 'boys' who were often abused by white soldiers and generally treated with disrespect. According to my mother, he brought his high-handed ways back from the war. He expected his children, for example, to blacken his boots or get 'no Saturday penny'. I remember her finishing this reminiscence with: 'Let him keep his bloody auld Saturday penny, that's what I thought.'

The former sergeant of the Connaught Rangers, who knew how to handle 'natives' and hold India by the sword, is likely to have been the kind of husband who wanted his own way. Yet I never heard my mother accuse him of drunkenness or violent abuse. Paradoxically, the stories of violence relate to Sally, who was a quick-tempered woman, prone to lash out when frustrated or challenged. My mother remembered her on one occasion when doing the weekly wash. This was always a time of trial and tension for the tenement housewife. There was heavy bedding to be carried up and down stairs and an exhausting day of work in the steam and wet of the communal washhouse, situated in the back court. For some reason, her son Joe got on the wrong side of his mother and she kicked out at him with the heavy, wooden-soled clogs she wore for splashing in and out of the wet. 'You should have seen the marks she left on his forehead,' my mother said.

Sally's temper did not improve, and she bequeathed to my mother an over-readiness, as it seems to me, to settle arguments by the use of force. 'Don't think you're too old to get a leathering,' my mother told me when I was perhaps ten or eleven. 'My mother broke a plate over my head for cheeking her, and I was nearly twenty-one at the time.'

With a wife like Sally, it would be a brave man who tried to get his way by the threat of force. That Willie might have tried at some time is suggested by another memory of my mother. On hearing of some young woman whose husband was abusing her, she commented in my hearing:

'What the hell's wrang wi' women these days. If he tried that wi' me, I'd lift something and gie him it ower the heid.'

But Willie, as we shall see, found other ways to repay Sally's resentments.

* * * * * *

The date of the Pattersons' removal to Clydebank cannot be established with certainty. They were certainly there in 1924, as can be seen from the records of Clydebank High School where their eldest child, Joe, commenced his secondary education. The same records confirm that they had been living in Clydebank for some time before that, since Joe transferred from Whitecrook, a local primary school. The date of their removal may have been 1921 when Willie, according to his Post Office record, was re-established as a civil servant. This almost certainly marks his promotion from the grade of postman to that of sorting clerk/telegraphist. At long last, the ambition to advance on the basis of his military qualifications seemed to have been realised. His wage scale as a postman stopped at 25 shillings. His new post was on a scale that rose to 32 shillings.

But these were not propitious times. The independent burgh of Clydebank, standing downstream from Glasgow on the north bank of the river Clyde, had fallen on evil days. Its shipyards had been renowned before the war for building world famous liners but, in the post-war depression of 1921, shipbuilding collapsed and Clydebank shared in the debacle. Unemployment in the industry climbed to forty-four percent by 1923 and wages dropped to nearly half the level they had gained before the depression.

Depression in Clydebank seems to have had a radicalising effect on the Pattersons. During these years, the Burgh had the severest housing problem in Scotland. House building had ceased during the war and the in-flow of workers to the shipyards, boosting armaments production, would have pushed rents up to scarcity levels if rents had not been pegged by government control. In 1920, however, faced with pressure from landlords, the Conservative-dominated coalition relaxed control and large rent increases were demanded on Clydeside. As unemployment soared in the shipbuilding industry, Clydebank became the main battleground of working-class resistance to increases. A powerful Housing Association was formed. It fought successful battles in the courts against rent increases. Meanwhile David Kirkwood, a war-time strike leader, had been elected to Parliament for Labour in 1922 and began warning of revolution if nothing were done about unemployment and housing. In Clydebank, a tenants' vigilante committee was formed to resist evictions under new legislation in 1923. Unemployed workmen toured the Burgh on bicycles, watching for the approach of eviction officers. Women rang bells to summon neighbours to block the streets and closes against them. Furniture seized by bailiffs for non-payment of rent was immediately seized by the crowd and returned to its owners. In 1924, the election of a minority Labour government failed to quell this unrest. It fell after only nine months and the ensuing Conservative government introduced changes in the law which finally permitted landlords to carry through evictions, free from effective challenge in the courts.

These and other events earned the region the name 'Red Clydeside'. The term is now regarded by many historians as misleading. It was coined by a hysterical press, which seemed to believe that Russian Bolshevism had captured the Clyde. In truth, wives of unemployed men simply could not pay the new rents, but there was little support for out-and-out revolution in Clydebank during the 1920s. The Clydeside Independent Labour Party aimed at Socialism by parliamentary means, though warning that revolution would be the result of ignoring its programme.

Yet the term 'Red Clydeside' is a useful one for drawing attention to the dramatic turn to the left which politics took between 1918 and 1924. The Scottish Socialist and future Prime Minister, Ramsay MacDonald, skilfully harnessed the militancy and frustration of the working people to build himself up as the leading parliamentary socialist in succession to Keir Hardie. Widespread discontent over housing also helped to return David Kirkwood as MP for Clydebank in 1922, together with James Maxton, John Wheatley and eight other Glasgow Independent Labour Party candidates.

In the midst of all this public drama, the Pattersons moved towards the ILP. At this distance in time, it is impossible to reconstruct the process with precision, though my mother often spoke of the family's ILP connections. It would be very interesting to know why a man like Willie moved from a background of militarism and imperialism to one of peace and international socialism. In the absence of his own direct testimony, however, we can only speculate. We can also guard against the temptation to set too high a store by it. It may not have been as far reaching as it could be made to seem.

Willie had fought for King and Country in a war from which Britain had emerged with a larger Empire and a victor's crown. The war time leader, David Lloyd George, had promised 'homes fit for heroes to live in'. Yet Willie and Sally found themselves living above the Post Office at number 10 Chalmers Street, Clydebank, in a cramped room and kitchen, with three growing children. Men like Willie, intelligent and ambitious, had seemed poised to inherit the new civilisation of the twentieth century – a world of wireless and telephones, of airplanes and motor cars. Yet all this had come to naught in the west of Scotland. To be sure, a local captain of industry, Sir William Beardmore, had launched into the new technologies after the war, only to fail for lack of government support. It may well have seemed to Willie that Scotland's share of the prize had been snatched away. The politicians had turned their backs on the new world and lost their grip on the old.

1930s Dole queue in Clydebank (© West Dumbartonshire Council Central Library)

Men like Willie might well have agreed with the Clydeside ILP leader, John Wheatley, who wrote to Beardmore pleading for continued investment in the new industries. More generally, people in the ILP often dreamed of the future which Edward Bellamy, the American Socialist, had predicted in his book *Looking Backward*. It was scientific and free from conflict. My mother certainly knew and admired it. 'Read *Looking Backward*, son,' she would say to me, years later.

But it is also possible that Willie's conversion to ILP politics had a more self-interested side. However proud of his advancement in the Post Office, he could not have disguised from himself that it had come too late. The telegraph was now in decline, confronting the telephone as the more modern means of communication. True, it still had a place wherever the printed word was more convenient, as in journalism, but it was definitely in retreat and the wages of male telegraphists stagnated. They were partly pegged back by the advancement of female telegraphists, whom the Post Office unions had resented ever since 1866. Many skilled working men, and Willie was one, regarded women as creatures naturally formed for men's comfort – wives who kept the home fires burning. For many such men, socialism was a rather patriarchal affair, developed in a labour movement dominated by men. They wanted industrial recognition and housing for their families, but wives and daughters would always be second-class subjects to them.

As to ideas, the socialism of Robert Blatchford may have touched Willie more closely than that of any other propagandist. Manny Shinwell, one of the Clydeside MPs and Willie's near contemporary, recalled how the writings of the ex-soldier, Blatchford, influenced his early thinking far more than the religiosity of Keir Hardie.

In *God and My Neighbour*, Blatchford taught that man is a product of heredity and environment. As such, he could not be blamed for committing immoral or illegal acts, though he might be pitied and in some circumstances forcibly restrained. He mocked Christians for their denunciation of sin. Logically, they should denounce God for having created fallible men:

> *If God made Adam weak, and Eve seductive, and the Serpent subtle, was that Adam's fault or God's? Did Adam choose that Eve should have a stronger will than he, or that the Serpent should have a stronger will than Eve? No. God fixed all those things. God is all-powerful. He could have made Adam strong enough to resist Eve. He could have made Eve strong enough to resist the Serpent. He need not have made the Serpent at all.*[64]

Willie could have taken writing like this in a very different sense from that intended by Blatchford. He could have used it to give a colour of justification to conduct that was rooted in cynicism and masculinity. Unhappiness, such as his and Sally's, was the product of bad laws, bad economics and bad material conditions. Sergeant Patterson was no more to blame than Sergeant Blatchford.

---

[64] *R Blatchford, God and My Neighbour (London, 1903) p. 134*

And what of Sally? Her later outlook in politics, of which I gleaned something from my mother, may suggest that she had also been radicalised, though perhaps in a different way. While Willie had been absent at the war, fighting for King and Empire, she had lived through the agitation in 1917 and 1918 for a negotiated peace. She sympathised warmly with her daughter who, in the 1930s, became an ardent opponent of 'warmongers' and 'imperialists'. With fervid internationalists like Maxton leading the ILP, she had her own reasons for inclining towards the ILP. Her allegiance to formal Christianity weakened and she allowed my mother to attend, at Willie's behest, the local Socialist Sunday School, where she learnt such 'commandments' as:

> *Do not think that those who love their own country must hate and despise other nations, or wish for war, which is a remnant of barbarism.*[65]

But Sally was not ready to break with Christianity completely and insisted that little Margaret also attend a church Sunday School, where she acquired a burning zeal to go as a missionary to Africa and convert 'black babies'.

* * * * * *

Whatever their agreement – or disagreement – in politics, the Pattersons were not to settle down companionably in their Chalmers Street home. Tension grew between Sally and Willie over the matter of Joe's future. Clydebank High School was renowned throughout Scotland for the number of pupils who proceeded to University. These were often boys who came from quite poor families and my mother's reminiscences blamed Willie for refusing to countenance Joe's 'staying on' at school to scale the educational ladder. According to my mother's account, Joe was a bright lad, nominated 'Dux' of his class in his last year at the school. He should have stayed on past fourteen to take the Higher Leaving Certificate, but the family would have had to

---

[65] F Reid, *Socialist Sunday Schools in Britain, 1892-1939, Int Rev Soc Hist, xi, 2, (1966)46*

pay for books and other fees and Willie, said my mother, preferred to keep his money for dancing and womanising. While, as we shall see, the charge of womanising is true, it is certain that Willie's Post Office earnings could not have financed Joe's further education without inordinate sacrifices. Thirty-two shillings a week in regular wages was a great deal better than unemployed men could expect to get, but it was not a large wage. True, it might have been possible to have seen Joe through to the end of secondary schooling and the Higher Leaving Certificate, but further education for the boy on Willie's earnings would have been practically out of the question. The future television vet, Eddy Straighton, son of working-class parents who attended Clydebank High School just a little later than Joe, recalled how the help of a tradesman uncle was necessary to get him through the Veterinary College in Glasgow, and then only by dint of very severe economy on his and his parents' part.

Willie might have taken the view, as many working-class fathers did in those days, that university education was a frill that his son did not need, and for which he should not be asked to sacrifice. Instead, he proposed that Joe should join him in the Post Office, starting at the bottom as a telegram boy. It would be the lowest rung of a secure career that might lead, as in his own case (perhaps much more quickly) to clerical employment and a respectable standard of living. Sally, on the other hand, was, no doubt like my mother, convinced of the intrinsic value of education and willing to make almost any sacrifice for the benefit of her son.

It was against this background that tragedy struck. Joe began working as a telegram boy out of Clydebank Sub-Post Office in 1926. One morning he had to deliver a 'wire' to Rothesay Dock, a great basin for the handling of coal and other minerals of which the burgh was extremely proud. According to my mother's recollection, Joe rushed into the dock with his telegram and shot over the wall into the water. A workman dived forty feet from above and tried to save him, but the bike pulled him quickly into the dark, dirty depths.

Recollected at this distance of time, the tragedy prompts a reflection on the stability of long-term memory. Many people can recall dramatic events which occurred directly in early experience with remarkable accuracy. My mother was no exception. I heard her tell this story of the uncle I never knew, over and over again from early childhood, and I wrote the preceding account from memory, recalling my mother's words as faithfully as I could. My daughter then traced the following report of the tragedy in the Clydebank Press of 23 July 1926. There could scarcely be more eloquent testimony to the substantial accuracy of my mother's recall (and my own, for that matter):

Rothesay Dock Tragedy: Telegram Boy Drowned

Considerable excitement was caused in Rothesay Dock, last Thursday morning, when Joseph Paterson [sic] (14) 10 Chalmers Street, fell from his bicycle into the dock. The lad had been cycling along the dockside to deliver a telegram at one of the ships when the accident occurred.

Gallant efforts at rescue were made by William Yule, boatman, 25 Clyde Street, and David Clark, traffic clerk, 9 Garriochmill Road, Glasgow, the last named diving from the dock side, a height of almost forty feet. Owing, however, to the dirty state of the water the rescuers were baffled in their attempts, finding it impossible to obtain a sight of the boy. About ten minutes after he had fallen in, two policemen succeeded in bringing the lad to the surface with the first throw of a grappling iron, but although they applied artificial respiration for fully an hour the boy never regained consciousness. A sad feature of the affair is that deceased was only relieving the regular telegram boy who is on holiday.

The records of Clydebank High School add poignancy to the last sentence of the report. Joe had not officially left school when he met his death and was no doubt standing in for a regular telegram boy as a means of introducing him to the postal service.

Joe's death must have embittered relations that had already been strained by recrimination. Some husbands might have sued for peace, appeasing the injured wife and smoothing things out over time. This was not Willie's way. The pioneering feminist, Mary Wollstonecraft, would have felt that Willie Patterson exemplified her low opinion of soldiers as callous seducers and dangerous despots in their homes. Not only did he openly 'run aboot the [dance] halls' (as my mother put it) with other women but, on at least one well-remembered occasion, he had the effrontery to bring a girl friend home for tea before taking her out dancing! Margaret often recalled her mother's outrage on that occasion. When tea was over, my grandfather rose to depart for his night's fun. Sally, her great eyes blazing with anger, jumped up from the kitchen table and crossed to the cooking range, where a coal fire was burning. Silent and seething, she pulled out the ash pan beneath. It was brim full and very hot.

She strode from the kitchen to the window of the back room, overlooking the close mouth at the foot of the tenement stairway. As they emerged in their finery – Willie dapper in shining black boots and spotless white spats – she lifted up the window and tipped the contents of the ash pan all over them.

We children used to laugh uproariously at this tale and our sympathies were with Sally, as anyone's must be. But a novelist might see the darker thread of tragedy, or at least pathos, that was beginning to weave itself into Willie's life. Victim of the venereal disease to which military regulations had exposed him at a tender age, hero of Empire who returned to a shattered Scottish society, rejected by his wife after two years of hardship at war – he must have felt bitterly estranged in the home to which he had returned. Only this seems to account for such a shocking act of mental cruelty as that of a husband who openly tries to humiliate a wife in the manner just narrated. There can be no excuse for Willie, but there may be some understanding.

* * * * * *

Sally's marriage seems to have reached breaking point somewhere around 1930, after my mother's fourteenth birthday, for I recall her telling how she had to leave Clydebank High at that time and go to work in Castlebank Laundry. Her elder sister, Sadie, was already working in domestic service. Sally now decided to leave Willie Patterson. In effect, as things turned out, she cut him out of her life and that of her descendents, and, in a sense, his story ends here. Yet I must go on with the rest of Sally's life in Willie's absence, since those were the years that shaped my mother's view of him, the view which I inherited.

Sally's was a very brave decision for a working-class woman to take in those days, but she knew that she could support herself and two daughters by working as a midwife. We may wonder how a woman like Sally acquired the knowledge and skill to perform such work. State promoted training of midwives had been introduced in Scotland in 1915, but it was still possible to assist at confinements on the basis of knowledge informally acquired by intelligent, hard-working and sympathetic women. Sally's name does not appear in the list of registered midwives that can still be consulted at Glasgow University, but she must have taken her calling seriously, for my mother recalled learning 'the facts of life' from her books, openly available on the shelves at home. Marion Robertson, my mother's lifelong friend, confirms my own memory of her recollections, in which Sally stands out as a strong and reliable nurse, much sought after for attendance at confinements. Most children were born at home and a doctor had to be paid for attending, either directly from the family purse or from savings in a thrift club. Consequently, he was called in only for difficult cases. Women would ask for 'Mrs Patterson', Marion recalls, 'to see them through a safe delivery with as little intervention from the doctor as possible.'

How then did Sally acquire these skills? It is probable that her connection with the United Presbyterian Church played some crucial part. Members of that denomination helped to lead the Scottish Calvinists towards the new 'social gospel' at the opening of the twentieth century. Lord Provost Chisholm was one of them. He played an important part in housing improvement in Glasgow. According to the new theological ideas which he embraced, sin sprang more from poverty and squalor than from man's fallen nature. Chisholm and his friends argued that the city corporation should provide a clean and healthy environment, leaving the churches to improve morality. From the earliest years of the twentieth century, the 'UPs' took a leading part in visiting working-class families, teaching basic rules of hygiene in maternity and child-care. It is not fanciful to think that this was the foundation of Sally's interest in nursing and midwifery. Her strong practical nature nourished the seed and the mature skills stood her in good stead when she needed to earn her own living.

Clydebank Public Library, 1998 (Mrs Margaret McQuire)

So it came about that, when life with Willie Patterson became unbearable, Sally took her daughters to live with her in a 'single end' at 132 Rottenrow, in the Townhead district of Glasgow, thus returning almost to the same area from which she had departed on her marriage.

A 'single end' was a one-roomed house, suitable for habitation by a single person or childless couple. Glasgow had more of such dwellings than any other city in Britain. As most of them were occupied by families, they contributed greatly to the overcrowded housing that was a by-word for Glasgow. Although I never entered the single end in Rottenrow (Sally being dead before I was born), I can readily imagine it, for my cousin grew up in one and I frequently visited her there during my boyhood. You entered from the 'landing' by an outer door which gave into a tiny vestibule, hardly big enough to remove your coat in. A door opposite admitted you into a small square room, which seemed so full of furniture that there was hardly any room to move about. The family had to do almost everything in this space eating dinner from the table, sitting round the fire on the sofa or one of the two armchairs, sewing at the machine by the window. There was barely enough room to open the great chest of drawers that held the clothes, table and bed linen.

Cooking and washing up were undertaken in a tiny scullery off the room. Everything was stowed away tightly in it, like a ship's galley – cupboard and cooker against one wall, sink and drainer against another, every surface festooned with hanging pots and cooking implements. There was barely enough remaining space to turn round in.

In the room, there was a 'press' or large cupboard in which the family possessions were stored. At night the parents and children slept in two double beds. These were housed in two 'recesses', three-sided spaces, one beside the scullery, the other beside the tiny entrance hall. Curtains were sometimes hung over the front of each recess to give a modicum of privacy to the sleepers.

The toilet was a water closet on the 'landing' which was used by three households. There was running cold water in the single end from a tap in the scullery, but all water for cooking, cleaning and bathing had to be heated on the gas cooker. If it rained on washing days, wet clothes had to be dried on a pulley that hung from the ceiling. Baths were taken in a tin bath in front of the fireplace.

In such a single end, Sally raised her two teenage daughters. She had to work hard to keep them. A woman who walked out on 'her man' in those days was neither welcome nor well provided for. The Rottenrow where they set up house was one of the oldest streets of Glasgow, close to the cathedral. More significantly perhaps for Sally, it was hard by the maternity hospital. Contact with 'The Mat' may have been a reason for taking accommodation there. There was another advantage in the proximity of Sally's sister, Mary. Mary was doing well and lived up a 'wally close' in nearby Cathedral Street. A wally close had the walls of the close and stairs covered by wall tiles – 'wallies' – and was considered far superior to the dark green and brown painted closes and stairways of the average tenement. I often visited Auntie Mary's house in my boyhood and marvelled at the coloured glass in her front door, the large number of rooms in her house and the hot water that gushed from the tap to fill the bath in her toilet.

Auntie Mary was a spectacle in herself. She weighed eighteen stone and seemed never to leave her armchair in the kitchen where she sat under a huge copper tank mounted on the wall to store all the hot water. My mother remembered her, however, as a tough old matriarch, who used to have the wage packets of all her working children thrown into her aproned lap each Saturday night, as one after another came home from work. The widowed mother of a large family, she had known hard times, but she pulled through, partly supported by her own mother, and partly by her eldest son, Robert Wright. As a youth, he had borrowed a hundred pounds from his grandmother (I have no idea how she came to have such a sum) and with it purchased a horse and cart. He went into the haulage business, carrying fruit to the market in the Candleriggs in the City Centre. By the time of my boyhood, he had built up the largest fruit contractor's business in Glasgow and I used to boast to my school friends that 'Robert Wright and Sons', whose trade name blazed from so many motor lorries, was 'my mother's cousin.'

They never believed me, and you could hardly blame them. How could her cousin be so rich and her living in a room and kitchen in Dundas Street, they asked? It was a question I could not then answer, but I gradually learned that Robert had disapproved of Sally and my mother. He was scornful of Margaret's Socialist views, but at en even deeper level he seems to have been uneasy with a woman who was so outrageous as to walk out on her husband.

Auntie Mary, for whatever reason, gave her sister's family little help in financial terms, but she did provide a second home in which Sadie and Margaret could find shelter and company when Sally went away to nurse her overnight cases.

* * * * * *

The records of Clydebank High School show that Margaret left on 31 January 1931. The date marked a decade that she would always refer to as 'the days of the depression', for it lived in Scottish memory like the seven lean years of famine in biblical Egypt. The New York Stock Exchange had collapsed in 1929 and the worldwide shock effects accelerated the decline of Scotland's heavy industry. Coalmines and shipyards fell silent and long lines of unemployed men queued for 'the dole' at the 'broo', as Scots called the Labour Exchange or Bureau. The streets of Clydebank were 'a melancholy sight' – 'crowds of men loafing about the whole day long', one eyewitness noted.

In some ways, the depression was not as bad for young women as for men. The latter found it hard to get apprenticeships in a region so heavily dominated by depressed industries. But the well-to-do still enjoyed their luxuries and shops staffed mainly by women. So were laundries and Margaret had gone to work in the Castlebank Laundry. The work was not too over-taxing for a strong young woman like her. The owners of Castlebank were noted philanthropists and men did the exhausting work of the steam washhouse. Margaret was employed at finishing work such as steam ironing and the hand washing and starching of fine shirts. Here she learned skills that stood her in good stead in the 1960s, when she, in her turn, walked out on her man and supported herself by managing various laundries.

It was at this time that she made lifelong friendships with young women like Marion Robertson and entered wholeheartedly into Socialist politics. There was an understood course of progression from the Socialist Sunday School into the Independent Labour Party Guild of Youth. Margaret duly joined up, but the Guild was losing prestige in the thirties to the more militant Young Communist League. For one thing, the Guild was tarnished by the weak response of the Labour government of 1929-31 to the mounting economic crisis and the collapse of sterling. Jimmy Maxton denounced Labour's leader, Ramsay MacDonald, after he resigned and formed a coalition with the Conservatives to defend the pound. He also attacked those Labour ministers in MacDonald's government who were forced to confess that they had been willing to cut unemployment benefit as a means of keeping sterling pegged to the Gold Standard. Maxton persuaded the ILP to break away from the Labour party and took a large following in Clydeside with him.

Margaret admired Maxton and treasured all her life the photograph taken with him and a group of young Socialists at an ILP dance but she was also getting to know the fiery young 'YCL'ers' who often joined the Guild of Youth crowd at the Socialist Sunday

School's summer camps at Carbeth. To this hillside near Clydebank, which Allan Barns-Graham let out at low rents for weekend huts and camping, the rebel youth of 'Red Clydeside' hiked and cycled each weekend. There was a lot of 'clean fun' – so Margaret said – and a lot of political argument. The Labour party was finished, the YCL'ers said. It had betrayed the working class and the Communist Party would have to be built up to take its place. This meant denouncing the trade union leaders who had sold out to the bosses, and supporting the unemployed in militant demonstrations against the means test. It also meant supporting the Soviet Union, which was building Socialism on planned lines. Marxism predicted that the next crash in the capitalist world would be the last one. Workers' revolution would be the only means of resisting Fascism, which had taken over in Italy and Germany and was growing in Britain and America.

Margaret and her two friends began to move towards the YCL position. I do not think that it was economic hardship that took her into the Communist Party. Her mother had to struggle as a separated lone parent, but, though 'things were tight', they were not living in abject poverty. The suffering of unemployed people under the means test moved Margaret to lasting anger, but the threat of Fascism soon added to her sense of outrage. According to Marion, Margaret's move towards the YCL along with herself began with the outbreak of the Spanish Civil War in 1936. Those were their years of war and romance. Young men who had been close friends joined the International Brigade and left Scotland to fight for the Spanish Republic against Franco and Fascism. An 'Aid for Spain Committee' was formed in Glasgow and the friends threw themselves into collecting tins of condensed milk – fresh milk was scarce in Spain. They also undertook to write regularly to the International Brigade lads out there.

My mother often said she was enjoying life too much to think of marriage at this time. Sally kept an open door for all her friends. In summer there was hiking and camping. In the winter there was political activity and the dances at the Workers' Club. Marion recalled that The Club met in a set of rooms above the Communist bookshop, Collets, then located at the corner of George Street and High Street in the Townhead. Sally had a 'wee job' running catering for it on a Saturday night. Several of the men fancied Margaret. According to Marion there was 'a wee boilermaker'. I remember a photograph she used to have among her collection which showed her eating an *al fresco* meal outside a tent with a man I did not recognise. She used to let me play with her photographs to keep me amused as a toddler.

ILP dance. The author's mother: fourth row from front, eleventh from left in light-coloured dress (Mrs Catherine Raeburn)

'That was my boyfriend,' she would say archly when I asked her who it was. But she was careful not to let any of them get too serious. One was a keen young Socialist who later became a leading left-wing Labour MP. He asked Margaret to marry him, but she turned him down, not (as he feared) because he was Jewish, but because she didn't care enough for him.

Yet life, as usual, had its darker side. Sally's elder daughter, Sadie, contracted tuberculosis. My mother worshipped her older sister. They went dancing together and Margaret thought Sadie a beautiful dresser. The three women grew to be close companions. Sally could still be young in spirit. 'Come on, hen,' she would say to Sadie, 'and teach me the modern dances' and they would foxtrot round the kitchen table.

But Sally was often absent now, nursing cases for a week or more at a time. One terrible day, which Margaret always remembered, she came home to find Sadie coughing up blood in the sink.

It was the 'galloping' form of the disease and Sadie was soon dying in a sanatorium. Margaret recalled how stoical she seemed in the face of death. When they visited her, she would point out the patients who were ready for 'the pan loaf.' The pan loaf was the grim name for the conveyance that came to remove dead bodies from the ward!

The death of Sadie in 1933, at the age of eighteen, was a second hammer blow for Sally. My mother always attributed it to Sadie's taste for the fast life. 'She would rush in frae work,' Margaret remembered, 'and rush out again tae the dancin'. If her knickers hadnae dried on the pulley, she'd put them on damp rather than be late.' But Sally, with some medical experience, may have known that Sadie's death had nothing to do with damp knickers. The truth was that Townhead was still a high-risk district for tuberculosis, despite the citywide improvements in public health that had been going on since the late nineteenth century. It has been shown that one hundred and forty people in every thousand died of the disease in Townhead in the 1930s. By comparison, in middle-class Pollokshields, with ample houses and spacious streets, the rate was fifty per thousand. It would have been surprising if Sally had not been tempted to blame herself. If she hadn't left the father, she must have agonised over and over again, and taken on this life of struggle to manage on her own, the girl might still be alive.

But her spirits rallied at times. She was even thought to be starting up a romance with a fellow in the Workers' Club. Then, in 1936, disaster struck. She became mysteriously ill, feverish and violently sick at times. It was appendicitis, but Sally was not at first alarmed. Dependent on her nursing for an income and unwilling to incur doctor's fees, she made light of her condition and tried to treat herself by 'poulticing' her stomach. This assuaged her symptoms for a time, but the pain always returned. As she grew more and more ill, she stubbornly refused all suggestions to call in a doctor. Margaret, worried almost out of her mind, finally sent for the doctor on her own account.

He sent her to hospital immediately where appendicitis was diagnosed, but it was not judged to be life threatening, or to require immediate operation. Suddenly her condition worsened when peritonitis ensued. There was an emergency operation, from which Sally never recovered. She died within a few days.

Margaret was devastated. I often heard her tell the story of that terrible time: how she had pleaded with Sally to get the doctor; how she had screamed at the hospital surgeon for not operating immediately. 'Miss Patterson,' he said, in the blunt language often assumed by authority at the time, 'we did not realize how bad your mother was until we put the knife in. She had been 'poulticing' herself so much that we thought she had only a grumbling appendix.'

But the family doctor told another story. Sally, he said, had lost the will to live, and this is what Margaret came to believe. In her mind, her strong handsome mother had been defeated by the cruelty of Willie Patterson. As she told and re-told the story of her early life, her father became the demon. She hated, with fierce contempt, the ostentatious grief he displayed over his wife's open coffin as it lay in the single end in the Rottenrow. Why had he gone with other women? Why had he lived such an unclean life? Why had he not been there for them when Sadie died?

From Margaret's point of view, contempt and rejection were inevitable and in some degree, justified. Yet Willie's grief over Sally's open coffin may not have been the idle tears of hypocrisy that she believed. They were, perhaps, the tears of a man who, like Thomas Hardy's Michael Henchard, the mayor of Casterbridge, sees his whole life as through a window pane and is forced to the conclusion that he has brought about the pain and suffering through his own actions.

Hardy, however, saw more deeply than his protagonist into the effects of Empire and war on the lives of men and society. I have argued elsewhere[66] that his great novel is set among the ancient remains of the Roman Empire in Wessex as a warning to his contemporaries that the 'New Imperialism' would produce a class of 'new barbarians'. The succession of Empires represented in his novel is a haunting threat that history may in fact be no march of progress, but a recurring cycle of civilisation and savagery. Men like Henchard, who cynically embrace the idea of a struggle for existence, and the 'new masculinity' that goes with it, will, given the appropriate circumstances, have the veil of self-deception rent from their eyes and experience a total estrangement from everything they try to build. Henchard's story must have been an analogue for many a 'soldier of the Queen' and the alienated words of Henchard's last will and testament might stand, with suitable alteration, as an epitaph for Willie:

> That ... [Margaret Patterson] ... be not told of my death, or made to grieve on account of me ... and that no man remember me.[67]

Henchard's daughter, Elizabeth-Jane, softened towards her father after his death: not so my mother. She never spoke to Willie again, passing him, from time to time in the street, without acknowledgment. As far as Margaret's family was concerned, the remainder of his life passed into oblivion. Historical records shed little light upon it. He retired early from the Post Office, on grounds of ill health, in 1939. The official record states that he 'discharged his duties with diligence and fidelity to the satisfaction of his superior officers' who recommended him for the award of the Imperial Service Medal. The practical outcome was that he obtained at last the pension he had long seen as due to him from the public purse.

Willie had gone on living in Clydebank and somehow survived the blitz of 1941. He died of a sudden heart attack, which struck him while travelling on a Glasgow bus on 13 July 1953. His death certificate shows that he was working, at the age of sixty-nine,

---

[66] F Reid, 'Wayfarers and Seafarers: Ideas of History in *The Mayor of Casterbridge*', *Thomas Hardy Journal*, 13.3 (1997)
[67] Thomas Hardy, *The Mayor of Casterbridge* (New Wessex edn, 1974) p. 353

as an insurance agent. No doubt, labour scarcity during the Second World War had enabled him to find a foothold in the clerical occupation that had not been available when he returned from India in 1910. It seems he had remarried. The second 'Mrs Patterson' reported the death and gave her previous surnames, curiously, as 'Helena McEwan or Martin'.

As we have seen, she exalted the status of Willie's father by recording him as 'china merchant deceased'. This little mark of snobbish pride has a rather poignant and regrettable significance, for it masks Willie's real and undeniable achievement: his upward mobility from the position of a semi-literate, unskilled labourer in the East End of Glasgow to the status of white-collar worker. We know all too little of such examples: how relatively rare they were, or how common; how exactly they were achieved. Willie's story deserves attention, not least for its value as a case study in the social history of Scottish working men.

Chapter Nine

'Strange Meeting'

'I am the enemy you killed, my friend.
... Let us sleep now ... '[68]

The writing of this book was undertaken in no spirit of ancestor worship. Rather, I was moved by curiosity, as many who wish to know more of their forefathers presumably are. Beginning in the style of personal memoir, I set out my recollections of the tales my mother told. According to these, her father was an utterly dishonourable person, who let his children down and drove his wife into an early grave. Never having known him personally, I was curious to know more of this black sheep. Faced with the commonplace records of genealogy, I began to ask definite questions which have been answered as far as possible in these pages.

How does Willie Patterson now stand in my eyes? The balance of judgment must surely be that he was rather better than the man my mother depicted and rather worse than the forefather I might have wished to celebrate. Yet Willie's story must go beyond a final account of virtues and vices. It raises some questions of general relevance to social history.

The introduction set them out. Social historians, for example, have often asked what motivated men of Willie's class to join up. Some stressed patriotic motives, but others have insisted on economic and cultural deprivation as the main factors pushing them into military service. Willie's story offers no conclusive evidence on this question, but tends to suggest that his motives were mixed. Joining the militia in 1900 may be seen as the act of a rather wild young man who turned to the colours as an escape from the narrow life of a Glasgow slum

---

[68] 'Strange Meeting', in *The Collected Poems of Wilfred Owen*, ed. C Day Lewis (London, 1963)

district and the cautious respectability of working-class self-help. His canny postponement of engagement in the regular army until the South African war was safely over may suggest that this was no 'death or glory boy'. Rather, he probably saw, or at any rate came to see, the army as an alternative road to self-improvement. His father had pursued white-collar status in civilian life with very limited success. The wild young man who was charged within the first few weeks of enlistment with drunkenness and swearing at an officer came, somehow, to see that further education and training in the army could offer a possible road to the kind of advancement his father sought and with, perhaps, more guarantee of success.

This is not the conventional view of the British 'Tommy'. Even the new social history of the Victorian and Edwardian army tends to stress the low status and under-achievement of the rank-and-file who were recruited from the city slums. Willie's story may suggest that there are other stories to tell. It may be that the issue should be re-visited and the private records and memories of families may have much to reveal about it. How many men learned a trade in the army? What happened to them afterwards in civilian life? How easy or difficult was their transition from military service? How many anticipated, like Willie, the demand for army pensions which, together with pay and separation allowances, became so marked a feature of ex-serviceman's grievances during and after the First World War?[69]

As to patriotism, Willie's history also seems intriguing. The Connaught Rangers certainly strove to instil in its men a spirit of service to the British Empire. The memoirs of its commanding officer, H F N Jourdain, if they are to be taken at face value, show a staunch commitment to death or glory:

> *When I think of death, as a thing worth thinking of, it is in the hope of pressing one day some well fought and hard won field of battle, and dying with the shout of victory in my ear – that would be worth dying for; and more, it would be worth having lived for!*[70]

---

[69] We know that at least one other did. Cp C Steedman, *The Radical Soldier's Tale: John Pearman, 1819-1908* (London, 1988)

[70] Jourdain, *Ranging Memories (1934)*, front inscription, attrib. Sir Walter Scott. Reprinted by permission of Oxford University Press

How many 'rankers' internalised such an outlook? It is hard to believe that it was very deeply imprinted in Willie Patterson. He had not entered the army contemplating death in a foreign field and, even in 1915, after quitting in a mood of disillusion, he made no voluntary effort to serve his country further in its hour of need. Indeed, as we saw, he waited until military service became compulsory for married men before returning to the colours.

But such life choices are rarely simple. If Willie viewed soldiering as a trade, it was a trade in which he was determined to do his duty to the best of his ability and he wished to be recognised for doing so. His grievance with the army was that it had twice failed him, first when its recommendation proved hollow and he ended up as a humble postman, instead of the white-collared telegraphist he aspired to be; and second when it turned down his offer to serve twenty-one years and become a pensionable soldier. Once re-engaged, however, the fortunes of war brought him recognition for 'conspicuous gallantry in action and devotion to duty'. The words must have seemed sweet and it seems harsh (or at least a-historical) to criticise the pride he took in the medals that hung above the fireplace at home in Scotland.

My mother probably misunderstood this pride. If Willie did see himself as a hero of the British Empire (as opposed to a soldier who had done his duty in arduous circumstances), he must surely have been disillusioned rather quickly. Scotland was in no sense a land fit for heroes after 1918. Not only did Willie personally return to humble service as a uniformed civilian, but he also had to wait for promotion to telegraphist until 1921. Promotion, when it came, was soured by the stagnation of the telegraph as a means of communication and by the blight of heavy industrial depression. His association with the Independent Labour Party was, almost certainly, an expression of this disillusionment, not with the cause of Britain and her Empire, but with the politicians who seemed to have lost the peace as surely as they won the war.

Willie must, then, have been a frustrated man in the post-war years, frustrated both in his public and private life. Frustration, in people of energy, often leads to acts of cruelty towards partners and family. Like Hardy's Michael Henchard, Willie probably came to see himself as trapped in a cage of circumstances and, being, like Henchard, a man with little more than a warrior's education, he reacted in a similarly confrontational manner. It is difficult not to condemn him, but judgment here is no less problematic for all that. Even today, in circumstances of easier divorce, the bitter loss that accompanies marital breakdown often makes people behave unconstructively. It was much harder in inter-war Scotland, to see any way out of such difficulties. Certainly, Sally seems to have been just as enraged as Willie and perhaps directed her rage into a degree of cruelty towards her children. She clearly helped to poison my mother's view of him. 'He thought he was the answer to a maiden's prayer,' she used to say, 'but he was the wrang bloody answer!'[71]

Perhaps the fairest way to sum up Willie is this: he had some heroic qualities and some tragic flaws which seem to have brought him a harvest of remorse and shame on the rather public occasion of his wife's funeral. Memory of the failings obliterated all trace of the determination and painfully acquired self-respect which had underlain his public achievements. This book may restore them to history.

* * * * * *

These conclusions have been reached by placing the known facts of Willie's story into various contexts of historical knowledge. By framing the events of his life in this way, I have been able to represent him as a more intelligible, though not necessarily a more sympathetic character than the reprobate my mother remembered. I like to think that she could have accepted this limited revision.

There remains one aspect of Willie's life, however, that she would have found great difficulty in appreciating – his military service in the First World War. My mother belonged to a generation that had come to look back on the war as unnecessary in its inception, futile in its outcome, pursued by politicians from motives of great power cynicism and imperialistic greed, and fought by generals devoid of any strategic plan beyond the slaughter of their men in a campaign of attrition.

---

[71] Information supplied by Marion Robertson

Until the 1960s and even beyond, the dominant trend in historical writing supported this view and popular representations of the War were built on such classics of lament and satire as *All Quiet on the Western Front* and *Oh What a Lovely War.*

Among a generation of historians that has grown up since the sixties, however, a very different view of the War has come to prevail. Far from being unnecessary, they see the First World War as vital to Britain's very existence against a ruthless and dangerous enemy. Not all of Germany's rulers acted with aggressive intent towards their European neighbours in 1914. Some saw themselves as responding defensively to a Russian threat, but once war broke out, the British knew that Germany's invasion of Belgium and France would give them control of the Channel ports, bases from which to launch her naval power and cut off access to the sea-lanes on which the British economy so largely depended. If the British wished to remain a great world power, therefore, they had no choice but to fight in 1914.

As to the huge losses of the conflict, the revisionists acknowledge the toll of suffering, but rescue the British generals from the charge of blindly sending their men to the slaughter. Little in their experience had prepared the generals for static trench warfare. To begin with, they over-estimated the power of artillery to 'soften up' the German defences and, in battles like the Somme, sacrificed their infantry to the deadly fire of German machine guns. Gradually, however, they learned to use the resources of modern warfare, such as airplanes, wireless and telephonic communications. The 'intelligence' thus acquired enabled them to direct their firepower with more deadly accuracy. Using guns, tanks, mines and infantry more scientifically, they finally achieved the goal of break-through in 1918.

Far from experiencing defeatism and despair, moreover, the British army as a whole maintained its morale throughout the war and never lost its collective determination to defeat the 'Hun', who had violated Belgian neutrality and attacked France.

Victory, when it came, was seen as the conclusion of a just war and the greatest feat of arms the British had ever achieved. As a recent historian[72] has reminded us, many, perhaps most British people, took that view in 1918. For many years afterwards, as the Cenotaph in Glasgow's George Square attests, people mourned the dead and the unprecedented numbers of losses involved, but were also proud that their fellow countrymen had fought like lions to save Britain and the civilisation for which she stood. Only a minority at the time felt that Empire was something shameful and most believed that 'backward' peoples in Africa and Asia were far better off under British than German rule.

* * * * * *

My mother, however, grew to maturity in the climate of disillusionment that grew up with economic depression and the approaching shadow of another global conflict. As a child in the twenties, she attended Socialist Sunday School, where she was taught to revere the memory of Keir Hardie as an opponent of militarism and colonialism. Graduating from Socialist Sunday School into the Independent Labour Party Guild of Youth, she became a passionate admirer of the ILP leader and anti-war crusader, James Maxton. One of her earliest memories, which she related to me, was of Maxton addressing a meeting in her parents' back court, standing on one of Sally's kitchen chairs. Many of the Scottish left had long followed Maxton in his detestation of the First World War as a futile abandonment of international order.

In this view they do not seem to me to have been wrong. As Hugh Strachan has recently suggested, belief in the outbreak of war as a calamity for European civilisation is not incompatible with recognition that victory over Germany was an achievement for British arms.[73] Few British people today could wish for the triumph of the Kaiser and the semi-authoritarian Reich over which he reigned, but it is possible to recognise at the same time that the war broke out because very few European politicians were prepared to make the sacrifice of pride that conciliation would have required. In this sense, the poet Wilfred Owen was faithful to one aspect of historical truth

---

[72] G Sheffield, *Forgotten Victory*: (London, 2001) pp. xi-xvi
[73] H Strachan, *The First World War, I*, xv

when he retold the story of Abram and Isaac as a parable of the outbreak of war:

> *Then Abram bound the youth with belts and straps,*
> *And builded parapets and trenches there,*
> *And stretched forth the knife to slay his son.*
> *When lo! An angel called him out of heaven,*
> *Saying, lay not thy hand upon the lad ...*
>
> *Offer the ram of pride instead of him.*
> *But the old man would not so, but slew his son,*
> *And half the seed of Europe, one by one.*[74]

Yet, when all this has been said, are we entitled to view Willie's martial pride as merely vanity in the last analysis? It is one thing to deplore Imperialism and great power conflict: it is another to deny the value of martial virtue and the profession of arms in itself. In each generation since 1914, there have been many who have hoped and worked for a world living under the rule of law. True pacifism apart, however, such ideals have had to recognise the threat of military force as a necessary sanction against law-breakers. In the 1890s, it was difficult for ordinary people in the major European states to be sure who the law-breakers were. British newspapers and politicians often denounced Germany as a flagrant interloper who insisted that might was right and initiated the 'scramble for Africa'. By the same token, Germans were often taught to see Britain's empire as the product of economic, naval and military force and to regard British homilies for free trade and international law as barefaced hypocrisy. Many 'men in the street', in Glasgow or Hamburg, came to take the simplistic, but not wholly unrealistic, view that the world was becoming a more lawless place in which other powers were trying to pull or keep their country down by force or the threat of force. It seemed to such people that the only intelligible reaction was to hope for peace and international order while preparing for war.

---

[74] Wilfred Owen, Collected Poems

Willie grew to manhood in a Scottish culture that shared this kind of ambivalence. Robert Burns, for example, could wear two different poetic masks on one and the same face. On the one hand, he could sing the praise of universal brotherhood:

> *For a' that, and a' that,*
> *It's comin' yet for a' that,*
> *That man to man, the world o'er,*
> *Shall brothers be for a' that.*

Many a Scottish 'pacifist' has raised his voice in unison, but failed to listen when the same poet celebrated Scotland's martial vigour:

> *But mark the rustic, haggis-fed,*
> *The trembling earth resounds his tread;*
> *Clap in his walie nieve[75] a blade,*
> *He'll mak it whissle;*
> *An' legs, and' arms,an' heids will sned*
> *Like taps o' thissle.[76]*

My mother was no stranger to this ambivalence. She passed in the thirties from the ILP Guild of Youth into the Young Communist League. Like most Communists, she was no pacifist. Support for the Spanish Republic and the International Brigade was one of the main issues that drew her into the YCL. Military resistance in a just cause was compatible for her with hatred of war as a product of economic and racial oppression. She saw no distinction between Fascists who crushed working-class organisation under the jack-boot, and British Imperialists who oppressed India at the point of the gun. All resistance to war – even warlike resistance – was, she believed, ethically correct, and workers' revolution would finally put an end to it. She could admire non-violent resistance, but believed that the oppressed must ultimately resist by force rather than be crushed. From her own point

---

[75] goodly fist
[76] lop off

of view, therefore, she could venerate Ghandi and Lenin at the same time.

So the daughter detested her father for military service in a shameful cause, while the father suffered the effects of diseases acquired in defence of British power. She banished him from her life and he withdrew into oblivion. Between them, however, there was a common ground, which she could never have admitted. The teenage laundry worker who passionately supported the International Brigade and Republican Spain was as keen on martial virtues as the father who doggedly did his duty against the 'brutes and braggarts' of the German Empire. Historical judgment cannot, in any final sense, condemn either as completely wrong. On this view of history, their descendents have at least this comfort: their ghosts can, after all, share some kind of strange meeting.

Note on Sources

Primary Sources
For the history of the Patterson family, see entries in the register of births, marriages and deaths and in the census of Scotland, 1881 and 1891, New Register Office for Scotland, Edinburgh. Records of births, marriages and deaths for Northern Ireland are obtainable through the General Record Office, Belfast. For information on Kilrea, Northern Ireland, see Kilrea Study Pack, Kilrea Public Library.
For connection of Joseph and Margaret Patterson with Calton United Presbyterian Church, see the Baptismal Register, 1875-1906, Mitchell Library, Glasgow CH3/332/5.
For the army service of Corporal William Flynn Patterson, see the following sources in the Public Record Office, London: Service record, WO 364/2876; award of Military Medal: the war diary of Divisional Troops, 1918, Royal Engineers, GHQ Signal Company, WO 95/5315 and war diary of Imperial Signal Company, Lindi, WO 95/5315.
For Portuguese entry into the war: CAB 37/144.
For British and Portuguese operations in East Africa, see especially report of General Jakob Van Deventer to Secretary of State for Foreign Affairs WO 158/476, and compare maps in WO 158/444 and telegrams in WO 158/464. Some additional information will be found in 'Extracts from Naval Papers Lindi June-Sep 1917', CAB 45/67 and 'Diary of Lt Col BARTON 3/1 KAR' CAB 45/58, Sep 1918.
For Willie Patterson's service in the Post Office: his 'Application for superannuation or other retiring allowance, approved on behalf of Treasury 2 December 1939', PO REF NO 86298/39, Post Office Archive, London.
For records of pupils attending Clydebank High School, inquiries should be directed to the school.

Oral Testimony
Interviews with Marion Robertson and May Hutcheson.

Secondary Sources
A full list of books and articles consulted cannot be given here. The following helped to form a general understanding of the 'Age of Empire'.
Bourne, J, *Britain and the Great War, 1914-18* (London, 1989)
Fage, J D and Oliver, R *The Cambridge History of Africa*, VI and VII (London, 1985)
French, D, *British Strategy and War Aims, 1914-18* (London, 1986)
French, D, *The Strategy of the Lloyd George Coalition, 1916-1918* (Oxford, 1995)
Hobsbawm, E J, *The Age of Empire*, 1870-1914 (London, 1987)
Judd, T, *Empire: The British Imperial Experience, 1765 to the Present* (London, 1996)
Louis, W R (ed), *The Oxford History of the British Empire, III and IV* (Oxford, 1999)
Oliver, R and Fage, J D, *A Short History of Africa* (6th edn, reprinted with postscript, London, 1995)
Sheffield, G, *Forgotten Victory: The First World War, Myths and Realities* (London, 2001)

Smith, I R, *The Origins of the South African War, 1899-1902* (London, 1996)
Strachan, H, *The First World War, I: To Arms* (Oxford, 2001)

The following were especially valuable for themes treated in the text:
Adler, M W, *ABC of Sexually Transmitted Diseases* (London, 1998)
Ballhatchet, K, *Race, Sex and Class under the Raj, 1793-1905* (London, 1980)
Bamfield, V, *On the Strength: The Story of the British Army Wife* (London, 1974)
Bartlett, T and Jeffery, K (eds), *The Military History of Ireland* (Cambridge, 1996)
Barton, J, *A History of Ulster* (Belfast, 1992)
Beckett, I, *The Amateur Military Tradition, 1558-1945* (Manchester, 1991)
Beckett, I F W and Simpson, K (eds), *A Nation in Arms: A Social Study of the British Army in the First World War* (Manchester, 1985)
Blatchford, R, *God and My Neighbour* (London, 1903)
Blatchford, R, *My Life in the Army: Daily Mail Novels* (London, 1910)
Blunden, E, *The Poems* (Braille edn London, 1930)
Bond, B (ed), *The First World War and British Military History* (Oxford, 1991)
Boyd, W, *An Ice Cream War* (London, 1983)
Breitenbach, E and Gordon, E (eds), *Out of Bounds: Women in Scottish Society, 1800-1945* (Edinburgh, 1992)
Brown, C, *A Social History of Religion in Scotland* (London, 1987)
Rrown, G, *Maxton* (Edinburgh, 1986)
Campbell, R H, *Scottish Shipbuilding: Its Rise and Progress* (London, 1964)
Campbell, R H, *The Rise and Fall of Scottish Industry* (Edinburgh, 1980)
Carson, J T, *God's River in Spate: The History of the Religious Awakening of Ulster in 1859* (Belfast, 1958)
Cecil, H and Liddle, B H (eds), *Facing Armageddon: The First World War Experienced* (London, 1996)
Clinton, A, *Post Office Workers: A Trade Union and Social History* (London, 1984)
Crossick, G, *The Lower Middle Class in Britain, 1870-1914* (London, 1977)
Daiches, D, *Glasgow* (London, 1982)
Davin, A, *Growing up Poor: Home, Street and School in London, 1870-1914* (London, 1996)
Devine, T M (ed), *Irish Immigrants and Scottish Society in the Nineteenth and Twentieth Centuries* (Edinburgh, 1990)
Dundas, Sir Charles, *African Crossroads* (London, 1955)
Farwell, B, *The Great War in Africa, 1914-1918* (London, 1987)
Fendall, C P, *The East African Force, 1915-1919: An Unofficial Record of its Creation And Fighting Career; Together With Some Account Of The Civil And Military Administrative Conditions In East Africa Before And During that Period* (London, 1921)
Ferris, J, *The British Army and Signals Intelligence During the First World War* (London, 1992) Flaubert, G, *Salambo* (Braille edn, London, 1941)
Fraser, W H and Maver, I, *Glasgow, II: 1830 to 1912* (Manchester, 1996)
Fraser, W H and Morris, R J (eds), *People and Society in Scotland 1839-1914* (Edinburgh, 1990)
Fussell, P, *The Great War and Modern Memory* (Oxford, 1992)
Gann, L H and Duigan, P, *The Rulers of British Africa, 1870-1914* (London, 1978)
Gann, L H and Duigan, P, *The Rulers of German Africa, 1884-1914* (Stanford, Ca, 1977)

Gifford, P and Louis, W R with the assistance of Smith, A, *Britain and Germany in Africa: Imperial Rivalry and Colonial Rule* (London, 1967)
Hanley, C, *Dancing in the Streets* (London, 1958)
Hardy, T, *The Mayor of Casterbridge* (New Wessex edn, London, 1974)
Heathcote, T, *The Indian Army, 1822-1922* (London, 1974)
Hodges, G, *The Carrier Corps: Military Labour in the East African Campaign, 1914-1918*, intr by Elspeth Huxley, (London, 1986)
Holcombe, L, *Victorian Ladies at Work* (Newton Abbot (1973)
Hoare, P, *Spike Island: The Memory of a Military Hospital* (London, 2001)
Holmes, R, *The Western Front* (London, 1999)
Hood, J (comp), *History of Clydebank* (Carnforth, 1988)
Hordern, C, *Military Operations: East Africa* (London, 1941)
Humes, W M and Paterson H (eds), *Scottish Culture and Scottish Education, 1880-1980* (Edinburgh 1983)
Hyam, R, *Empire and Sexuality: The British Experience* (Manchester, 1992)
Iliffe, J, *Tanganyika Under German Rule, 1905-1912* (Cambridge, 1969)
John, A and Eustance, C (eds), *The Men's Share: Masculinities, Male Support and Women's Suffrage in Britain, 1890-1920* (London, 1997)
Jourdain, H F N, *The Connaught Rangers* (3 vols, London, 1928)
Jourdain, H F N, *Ranging Memories* (Oxford, 1934)
Kernohan, J W, *A History of Two Parishes: Kilrea and Tamlaght O'Crilly* (Coleraine, 1920)
Kilrea Local History Group, *The Fairy Thorn: Gleanings and Glimpses of Old Kilrea* (Kilrea, 1984)
King, E, *The People's Palace and Glasgow Green*, (Glasgow, 1985)
Louis, W R, *Great Britain and Germany's Lost Colonies* (Oxford, 1967)
Macdonald, C M and McFarland E W, *Scotland and the Great War* (East Linton, Scotland, 1999)
Macfarland, E W, *Protestants First: Orangeism in Nineteenth Century Scotland* (Edinburgh, 1990)
Maclean, I, *The Legend of Red Clydeside* (Edinburgh, 1983)
Mangan J and Walvin J (eds), *Manliness and Morality: Middle-Class Masculinity in Britain and America, 1800-1940* (Manchester, 1987)
Miller, C, *The Battle for the Bundu* (London, 1974)
Newitt, M, *History of Mozambique* (London, 1995)
O'Sullivan, P (ed), *The Irish World Wide, History, Heritage, Identity, II: The Irish in the New Communities* (London, 1996)
Owen, W, *Collected Poems*, ed C Day Lewis (London, 1963)
Pelling, H, *Social Geography of British Elections, 1885-1910* (London, 1967)
Price, R, *An Imperial War and the British Working Class: Working-Class Attitudes and Reactions to the Boer War, 1899-1902* (London, 1972)
Priestley, R E, *The Signal Service and the European War of 1914 to 1918: France* (Chatham, 1921)
Proust, M, *Remembrance of Things Past, I: Swann's Way,* (Braille edn, London, 1966)
Reid, F, *Keir Hardie: The Making of a Socialist* (London, 1978)
Richards, F, *Old Soldier Sahib* (London, 1936)
Robbins, K, *Nineteenth-Century Britain: England, Scotland, and Wales, The Making of a Nation* Oxford, 1989)

Russell, J B, *Public Health Administration in Glasgow: A Memorial Volume of the Writings of James Burn Russell, ed AK Chalmers* (Glasgow, 1905)

Sassoon, S, *The Complete Memoirs of George Sherston*, (London, 1937, 1972)

Scotland, J, *The History of Scottish Education,* (2 vols, London, 1969)

Slaven, A, *Development of the West of Scotland, 1750-1960* (London, 1975)

Spiers, E M, *The Army and Society*, 1815-1914 (London, 1980)

Spiers, E M, *The Late-Victorian Army 1868-1902* (Manchester, 1992)

Steedman, C, *The Radical Soldier's Tale*: John Pearman, 1819-1908 (London, 1988)

Supple, B, *The Royal Exchange Assurance* (London, 1970)

Swift, H G, *A History of the Postal Agitation* (London, 1929)

Trustram, M, *Women of the Regiment: Marriage and the Victorian Army* (Cambridge, 1984)

Vaughan, W E (ed), *Ireland under the Union* (Oxford, 1989), *Volume I of A New History of Ireland* ed F X Martin et al

Von Lettow-Vorbeck, General, *My Reminiscences of East Africa* (London nd)

Wilson, T, *The Myriad Faces of War (London, 1986)*

Wollstonecraft, M, *A Vindication of the Rights of Woman*, ed with intro M Brody (first pub. 1792, Penguin Classics edn. London, 1985)

Articles

Devon, Dr J, 'The Calton Fifty Years Ago, Transactions of the Old Glasgow Club', VI, 3, 1930-31

Fyfe, P, 'A Tour in the Calton, Transactions of the Old Glasgow Club', III, 4, 1916-17, 267-80

Reid, F, 'Socialist Sunday Schools in Britain, 1892-1939', *International Review of Social History, XI, 1*, 1966, 18-47

Reid, F, 'Wayfarers and Seafarers: Ideas of History in *The Mayor of Casterbridge'*, Thomas Hardy J, XIII, 3, 1997, 47-57

Thompson, Col E S, 'A Machine Gunner's Odyssey through German East Africa: The Diary of E S Thompson' *J of S African Military Hist, VII*, 3-6, 1987)

Cualann Press Titles

The Lion and the Eagle: Reminiscences of Polish Second World War Veterans in Scotland
Editor: Dr Diana M Henderson LLB TD FSA Scot.
Foreword: His Excellency Dr Stanislaw Komorowski
ISBN 0 9535036 4 X … £9.99

Stand By Your Beds! A Wry Look at National Service
David Findlay Clark OBE, MA, Ph.D., C.Psychol., F.B.Ps.S.
Preface: Trevor Royle, historian and writer
ISBN 0 9535036 6 6 … £13.99

Open Road to Faraway: Escapes from Nazi POW Camps 1941-1945
Andrew Winton D A (Edin)
Foreword: Allan Carswell, Curator, National War Museum of Scotland
ISBN 0 9535036 5 8 … £9.99

Beyond the Bamboo Screen: Scottish Prisoners of War under the Japanese
Extracts from Newsletters of the Scottish Far East Prisoner of War Association and Other Sources
Tom McGowran OBE. Foreword and Illustrations by G S Gimson QC
ISBN 0 9535036 1 5 … Price £9.99

On Flows the Tay: Perth and the First World War
Dr Bill Harding Ph.D., FEIS.
Foreword: *The Times* journalist and author
ISBN 0 9535036 2 3 … Price £12.99

Under the Shadow: Letters of Love and War
The Poignant Testimony and Story of Hugh Wallace Mann and Jessie Reid
Foreword: Dr Diana M Henderson
Narrative: Bríd Hetherington
ISBN 0 9535036 0 7 … Price £12.99

Of Fish and Men: Tales of a Scottish Fisher
David C Watson
Foreword: Derek Mills
ISBN 0 9535036 3 1 … Price £10.99

Coasting around Scotland
Nicholas Fairweather
ISBN 0 9535036 8 2 … Price £12.99

Cualann Press: Email cualann@btinternet.com Website www.cualann.co.uk